ATOMS, MEN and GOD

ATOMS, MEN and GOD

by

PAUL E. SABINE

PHILOSOPHICAL LIBRARY
New York

PRINTED IN THE UNITED STATES OF AMERICA

CONTENTS

Preface

BEFORE committing himself to the reading of a book bearing so all-inclusive a title as this one, the prospective reader may well ask, "Just what is it about? What, if anything, is the author trying to prove?"

Many times during the almost fifteen years that the book has been in the manuscript stage, being intermittently written, revised, and rewritten, the author has asked himself these same questions.

I knew that I was not trying to prove any specific proposition, either scientific or religious. I knew definitely that I was not writing simply for the fun of writing. Writing has never been one of my favorite forms of indoor pastime. I finally decided that, in the laborious job of putting my then jumbled ideas on paper, I was doing what a scientist usually does when he has to make sense out of what seems like conflicting experimental data—namely, to write it all out and look at it objectively from different points of view. This is standard procedure in the attempted solution of a scientific problem, and that was what I was doing with a personal problem that had been bothering me during most of my adult life. It was like a small splinter under a thumbnail—annoying, but not sufficiently painful to warrant my taking any very decided measures to get rid of it.

My problem was one which I think many thoughtful Protestant Christians find troublesome today. Put as simply as possible the problem is this: "Can I be intellectually honest in believing what, as a Christian, I profess to believe and at the same time accept the teachings of modern science and psychology regarding the nature of man and God and the physical world?"

There were two reasons why the problem was important for my mental peace. There was first the fact of an emotional conditioning that came from a childhood in the home of a pioneer Methodist preacher. The religious atmosphere of that home was one of unquestioning belief in God as a loving Father and of faith in Jesus Christ as an everliving reality. That heritage was and is something not lightly to be cast aside.

Later came the effect of my scientific training. In college and in graduate school, while there was nothing that was in overt opposition to my youthful religious environment, yet the pervading atmosphere of so-called liberal thought provided little to strengthen or even sustain a religious attitude toward life and its problems. Whether or not there is in reality a conflict between science and religion, nevertheless there came in time to be a "cold war" between what I tried to believe on Sunday, and the generally sceptical attitude that the scientist is apt to assume toward any hypothesis or set of ideas that cannot be verified by scientifically valid processes.

Had I been a good Catholic the disposition of my problem would have been easy. As a scientific Catholic friend once said to me on the subject: "Why not thank God that we have in the Pope an infallible authority on all questions of faith and doctrine and dismiss the problem from your mind and leave it to the Church to solve?"

But having been born and reared in the Protestant tradition, this short cut to religious certainty was not for me. My problem was not so much a matter of open conflict between what I considered to be the *facts* of science and my inherited beliefs, but rather a lack of intellectual orientation in a field in which not only religion but science and philosophy as well lay claim to a certain measure of authority. In short, what I was after was a personal philosophy in which the world of science and the world of religious faith were not two worlds of thought, appearing as two separate realities, but rather as one world seen from two angles of vision. I wanted a way of thinking that would fuse the scientific image and the religious image of the reality back of sense impressions and conscious experiences into a single image having a three-dimensional perspective that neither the purely scientific view nor the purely religious possesses by itself. I wanted a pair of mental binoculars fitted with a scientific prism in one lens system and a religious prism in the other that would give a single, two-eyed vision of the physical and the spiritual aspects of the world of conscious experience.

It is a common practice among scientists to keep other scientists posted on what they are doing, and what they have done, by writing articles for the scientific journals. In this way all that is being done in a given field becomes common knowledge for all workers in the field. A published paper is somewhat in the nature of a progress report, and seldom contains any note of finality. It is open for appraisal and criticism on the part of the author's colleagues.

It is in this spirit that the following chapters are offered to serious readers who are finding intellectual roadblocks in their roads to assured religious beliefs. I make no guarantee that the reading of this book will remove those obstructions for the reader. I can only cherish the hope that in what I have written the reader may find suggestions that will help him to find passable detours around them.

My sincerest thanks are due to many friends who, by their sympathetic understanding and expressed desires for a book of this kind, have "spurred the sides of my intent" to the task of its writing. This is particularly true of my lifelong friends, eager searchers after truth, Ed and Margot Small. To Miss Helen Gauss and Miss Helen Phillips I am deeply indebted for expert help in making readable prose out of my lapses into involved sentences that all but fell apart of their own weight. I cannot refrain from expressing the deep gratitude that I owe my wife for her unfailing understanding and help in what has been in fullest measure a family enterprise.

That the manuscript survived a lapse of four years, in which a strenuous program of war research precluded all thought on the subject is due to the kindness of Dean Sperry of the Harvard Divinity School. My most sincere thanks are extended to him for the encouragement he gave me to revise the manuscript. Equal thanks go to Professor J. Glenn Gray of the philosophy department of Colorado College, who suggested certain changes in treatment desirable from the philosophical point of view, and for his generous help at all times.

PAUL E. SABINE

ATOMS, MEN and GOD

Chapter 1

The Common Ground of Science and Religion

"Science is one form of the ever-living cosmic evolution, but not the only form in which the underlying reality touches the minds of men."[1]

William Lowe Bryan

Modern man lives in two worlds of thought. In one, the world of atoms, he confronts a closed universe of matter and energy, an integrated ideological system devoid of all spiritual meanings. These meanings he must find in a separate world of moral and spiritual values. These values inhere in a belief in the existence of spiritual realities, not included in the categories of science, but comprising another closed system of their own. This latter belief springs from some sort of religious faith. In Christian thought, this faith centers in the idea of God set forth in the ancient Hebrew and Christian Scriptures and revealed in human terms in the life and teachings of Jesus of Nazareth.

Present day men and women of religious temper, a group to which this writer belongs, find living in this divided world of thought and feeling difficult and uncomfortable. For them a positive religious faith is essential to physical, mental and emotional health. Such a faith is difficult to develop and maintain in minds perplexed by intellectual doubt and uncertainty. It is well nigh impossible to find any grounds for believing in the God of Christian teaching in a physical world of terrifying atoms or in a human world dominated by hatred, strife and greed. Ours is a world of

[1] *Wars of Families of Minds,* Yale University Press, 1940.

moral and spiritual chaos that has all but destroyed faith in a supreme Power that makes for righteousness in the affairs of men.

It is to this group of possible readers who have a "will to believe" and are finding rough going in their search for a *way* to believe that the following pages are addressed. One can not hope to bring light in the darkness nor to create order out of chaos. The best any one of us can do is to work out his own individual solution of a problem that vexes the minds of many thinking people, and, if he has the temerity to think that solution may have value for others struggling with the same problem, to present it to them in ordered form. That is what is attempted in the following pages.

The problem is more than an academic one. For the writer it has long been an acute, personal problem, and some sort of a solution has been essential for that "peace of mind" we are all seeking. Simply stated it is this: "Can I be intellectually honest while holding my inherited religious beliefs and at the same time accept the teachings of modern science and psychology about the nature of the world and of man?"

The easy solution is one that practically begs the question. It is to the effect that believing in God involves an entirely different mental process from believing in the atoms. That puts the dividing line between the two worlds of thought right down the middle of the human mind and still leaves one in the schizoid state of feeling that the solution of the problem is presumed to relieve. Anybody who gives the matter any thought at all knows that he has only one mind and that it is not divided into watertight compartments. This solution leaves one still a divided being living in a divided world.

Another solution is that of radical scepticism which maintains that our ideas of the atoms correspond to real entities having an objective existence quite independent of human thought, whereas our ideas of God and the spiritual values that emerge from those ideas have no substratum of reality outside human consciousness.

Physical science starts with the fundamental assumption that the source of all sensory experience is self-existent matter. The scientist's job is to explore the world of matter in its myriad forms. In general, the man of science considers this a full time job and thinks of the question of the relation of his world of material atoms to the world of spiritual values and meanings as being outside his scientific bailiwick. On religious matters his grounds for belief or disbelief are the same as those of any other thoughtful person. His qualifications for making final judgments outside the scientific field are no better than those who do not have his scientific background.

However, it is fairly safe to suppose that if a scientist has any religious interests whatever, the very fact of his scientific training will make the problem of the two worlds one of primary importance in his thinking as an individual. Intellectual honesty is an essential quality of the scientific mind and integration of his religious beliefs with his scientific concept of the nature of the world will be a matter of deep concern in the scientist's personal philosophy. He feels that the world view of science should encompass the whole field of human experience and therefore it becomes his duty as a scientist to fit whatever religious convictions he holds into the conceptual framework of science. It is the writer's experience that this is a job that requires quite a bit of doing. As a general rule, the working man of science is far too much engrossed with the immediate problems for which he can reasonably expect to find solutions to spend very much mental effort on one problem whose consideration he can postpone until he has reached the retirement age.

Hence, though the man of science may find the disparity between his religious and scientific credos a matter of personal concern, he may find it impossible to effect any kind of a fusion between his two worlds of thought. In this event it is the scientific picture that comes to occupy his entire field of vision, while he turns the problem of the interrelation between the religious and scientific meanings over to the philosopher and the theologian. If, by any chance, either of these has a solution to offer, it is apt to be presented in language that can not be translated into scientific terms.

Hence it comes about that while the individual scientist may not deny or even question the truth of religious teachings, yet professionally he ignores them as having no bearing on the kind of problems in which he is interested. Religion raises questions for which as a scientist he has no answers and no means of finding answers. Hence the attitude of modern science to the intellectual elements of Christian faith has come to be one of strict neutrality. Personally, the scientist may hold deep religious convictions. Many do. But these are personal and individual and are not implicit in the generally accepted tenets of the whole body of scientific teachings.

This elimination of all extraneous elements from the problem in hand is standard operational procedure in the purely scientific quest of truth. Admittedly, it gives what one may call a "one-eyed view" of the totality of experience, a flat two dimensional picture of the real world as it appears in human consciousness. But it finds full justification in the fact that it concentrates scientific endeavor upon problems that are amenable to scientific solution. Moreover it frees modern scientific thought from the metaphysical preconceptions and misconceptions that cluttered up ancient and medieval science. Like the "one-eyed" view that the microscopist gets of the specimen on his microscope slide, this monocular view of the physical world is reliable within its own self-imposed limits. It answers in its own terms questions of the *how* of physical events, but leaves the larger human question of *why* to those who undertake to interpret its findings. At this point the present day scientist leaves off and the philosopher and the theologian presumably take over.

If it is true that the attitude of the scientist toward religious teaching is one of strict neutrality, it is on the other hand equally true that most religious teachers of today do not come to grips with the troublesome problem of reaching and maintaining a rational religious faith in this age of the atom. Their solution of the problem of the two worlds seems not to be essentially different from that of the religiously minded scientist. They would maintain that since science is not religion and religion is not science, a mixture of the two is neither scientific nor religious. Let us suppose that a minister attends a popular lecture on nuclear physics delivered by a professor of physics who happens to be one of the minister's parishioners. He could very well say to himself, "what I understand of all this is interesting and doubtless true, but true or not, it has nothing to do with the religious truths that I shall proclaim in my sermon next Sunday". On Sunday, the professor listening to the minister's sermon may say: "I suppose that this is all true enough, but however true it may be it is not the same brand of truth that I shall teach my class in physics tomorrow".

By a sort of gentlemen's agreement, the parson and the professor each maintains his own ground and stays out of the other's territory. As a result, science forges ahead unhampered by any moral or religious restrictions, while religion, thanks to its amazing vitality, continues to survive in an intellectual climate that is anything but favorable to its potential growth. In this divided world of thought, it has come about that the material achievements of science and technology have captured the thinking of everyday men and women while the place of religion, insofar as it has any place in their lives, is in the realm of the emotions. We are all too sure of the *reality* of the atom, although in the mind of the layman there is no adequate conception of the nature of the reality that the word symbolizes. At the same time we may continue to believe in a reality that is symbolized by the word "God" but for many that belief is without assurance and the reality behind the word becomes increasingly problematical.

The modern concept of the material atom as a tremendously concentrated bit of radiant energy is the end result of three and one half centuries of development in physical science. With that development have come changes in all the external conditions of civilized life far more profound than all those that came in human history before the dawn of the scientific age. Even more profound are the changes that have come in our concepts of the world of stars and atoms. The stellar universe as conceived by the modern astronomer differs from that of Copernicus and Kepler far more than the modern theologian's idea of God differs from the tribal Jahveh of ancient Israel. The atom of the atom bomb is no more like the chemical atom of fifty years ago than the jet propelled airplane is like a baby carriage.

It is not surprising that these revolutionary changes in the outlook of modern man on his total physical environment should have produced equally revolutionary changes in the intellectual background of his religious beliefs. The single eyed view that the scientist, for his own particular purpose, takes of the world of external nature has come to be the total view of all human experience that much of philosophic and popular thought of today envisages. There is no place in a world of material atoms whose movements are controlled by blind electrical forces for the operation of a purposeful *will* either human or divine. Since this is the only world with which science is concerned and the only world with which it can deal and since science has the last word for the modern mind this must be the only *real* world. Carried to its logical conclusion this line of reasoning leads to a completely materialistic and deterministic philosophy. In secular thought, the atoms have preempted the place that earlier less scientifically minded generations assigned to God.

Although the older atomistic mechanism, as a complete account of the material world, has now been abandoned by physical scientists, nevertheless a materialistic philosophy still dominates, in large measure, the thought of our times. In such a philosophy, spiritual values and ethical ideals appear as entirely man-made, human inventions for the curbing and socialization of man's animal instincts, having no basis in the structure of the world. Moral codes and restrictions are purely relative to the cultures in which they prevail, with no universal validity beyond their utility in maintaining the particular cultures in which they have arisen. Human personality appears as the product of the secretions of the endocrine glands, and human conduct results from conditioned reflexes that are completely determined by the social environment of the individual. Hence the idea of personal, moral responsibility is completely illusory. The religious impulse is nothing more than a vestige of the superstitious fear of the primitive mind. The idea of God is at best a metaphysical abstraction, and belief in the existence of a Divine Will and Purpose, either in the ordering of an individual life or in the great movements of human history, must be characterized as the supreme illusion which modern man has not yet outgrown. The net result of all this is a pessimistic, fatalistic view of "this sorry scheme of things entire" whose practical result is either a stoical acceptance of things as they are, or a complete abandonment of moral and spiritual principles in favor of an "enlightened hedonism".

Now this dark view of things is only the modern version of a philosophy that is far older than modern science. No modern Existentialist could better express the feeling of the utter meaninglessness of the world of nature, which a mechanistic philosophy engenders, than did the Roman poet Lucretius in lines written a half century before the birth of Christ:

"Globed from the atoms, falling slow or swift
I see the suns, I see the systems lift
Their forms, and even the systems and their suns
Shall go back slowly to the eternal drift."

A present-day philosopher has recently summarized this general attitude in modern thought in a much discussed magazine article.[2] He maintains that "science has killed religion," and writes: "The world according to this new (scientific) picture is purposeless, senseless, meaningless. Nature is nothing but matter in motion. The motions of matter are governed not by any purpose, but by blind forces and laws." Further he says: "You can draw a sharp line across the history of Europe, dividing it into two epochs of very unequal lengths. The line passes through the lifetime of Galileo. European man before Galileo, whether ancient pagan, or more recent Christian, thought of the world as governed by plan and purpose. After Galileo, European man thinks of it as utterly purposeless." Still further he insists: "Belief in the utter irrationality of everything is the quintessence of what is called the modern mind."

There is undoubtedly a certain factor of correlation between the progress of science and the decline of Christian faith in Western culture. General acceptance of the "one-eyed" view that the total world of conscious experience is covered by the laws of physics and chemistry is bound to lead to the abandonment of a belief in the existence of a personal God who governs by divine fiat the world of men and things.

Equally lacking in intellectual perspective is the view of too many religious teachers that the age-old truths of Christian teaching can be couched in language that is meaningless to modern minds and still call forth the unqualified acceptance with which they were received by past generations. In every field of thought the last fifty years have seen

[2] "Man Against Darkness": W. T. Stace, "Atlantic Monthly", September, 1948.

a shift of outlook far more profound and far reaching than any that has occurred since Copernicus shifted the center of man's universe from the earth to the sun. The most profound shift has come in scientific thought. In the writer's opinion, an equal shift is still due to come in religious thinking.

In speaking of the shift of scientific viewpoint one is referring not so much to the epoch-making discoveries of the period as to the revolution in the fundamental processes of scientific thinking that these discoveries have brought about.

Nature has a disconcerting way of giving equivocal even contradictory answers to questions put to her in the language of experiment. These answers sometimes call for two mutually contradictory interpretations. We shall cite numerous examples in later chapters. In such cases science accepts both of two opposing ideas and regards them as partial expressions of a truth that is more inclusive and hence nearer the underlying reality than is either of the conflicting interpretations. A new concept emerges—not a mixture, but an intellectual synthesis of the earlier concepts. Modern science has arrived at this stage of development—the analytic process of earlier scientific thought is being replaced by a process of synthesis that reconciles the contradiction of earlier partial interpretations. The concepts of time and space, force and motion, energy and matter, waves and particles—all hitherto strictly defined so that each excluded all the others, have been merged in the comprehensive theories of Relativity and Wave Mechanics. In modern physics, each of these fundamental concepts is defined in terms of its relationships to the others. The world of physical phenomena has thus been reduced to one of mathematical relationships.

Now this new world of modern physical theory is essentially a mental image of the world of sense experience. It is a *creation* in a very real sense of the human mind. It creates a rational order out of the chaos of natural phenomena. It establishes a ground of mental realities for what we call "physical" facts.

But this new world view of science still presents as flat an image of the real world as did the older mechanistic view of inert matter and mechanical and electrical forces. While it imposes a rational order upon the happenings of external nature, yet it is still a closed system of mental realities that excludes the most significant fact of all, the human mind that has created it. To be sure modern physical theory includes the "observer" and the effect that the very fact of observation has on the sequence of the observed events. The "observer", however, is not a person, but only an electro-mechanical robot that by some means records the occurrence of a purely physical event. Physical science stops dead in the face of the supreme mystery, the mystery of human personality.

Here we find ourselves facing the age old metaphysical problem of the relationship between mind and matter. Modern physical science does not offer any solution of this problem, but it does put it into a form that will allow the scientific procedure of synthesizing mutually exclusive concepts into a single concept that is more comprehensive than either of its components. In the establishment of a mathematical world image, modern physics puts mental qualities into the ultimate structure of the physical universe. In so doing it makes legitimate, though perhaps not necessary, the belief that there is an intrinsic correlation between the processes of Nature and the process of human thought. This would imply a mental quality in the final structure of the world of which the mind of man is an individualized part. In fact, without being unscientific, one can believe that the stuff of the world is both physical and psychical.

In this approach to the mind-matter dilemma, we do not depart from the recognized scientific method of thinking. In substituting the words "both—and" for the words "either—or" we have followed the precedent of Relativity

Theory in synthesizing the traditionally separate concepts of space *and* time into the mathematically defined concept of "space-time". Wave Mechanics does the same sort of thing when it finds explanation for the puzzling behavior of the electrons, protons and neutrons in the mathematical characteristics of "wave-particles".

This brings us to the heart of the problem with which we are concerned. Is it possible or even reasonable, to carry this process of scientific synthesis still further and try to get a stereoscopic view of both the God-centered world of Christian faith and the world of the electrical wave-particles that will give an added dimension to both the religious and the scientific pictures of a final reality that includes both the spirit of man and the order of Nature?

One has to admit that even though an attempt to achieve this binocular vision may be scientifically justifiable, yet it does not follow that success in the effort would contribute in any degree to our purely scientific knowledge of the world of sense experience. Moreover, although modern physical theory unifies the processes of natural phenomena and those of mathematical thought, yet there is no place in its symbolic structure for the insertion of a term that corresponds to that which is symbolized by the term "God" in Christian teaching. For the new physics, as for Barthian theology, God must be the "wholly other". God, together with the creative mind of the scientist, exists wholly outside the "universe of scientific discourse".

But, as we shall try to bring out in later chapters, there is a profound difference between the modern mathematical world image and the atomistic mechanism of classical physics. In the older view, the physical universe was reduced to a vast cosmic machine set going somehow in the distant past and doomed to run down in the future. Its origin was considered to be an historic event which the pious mind of Newton ascribed to a single creative act of God. Beyond that one act of creation there was neither place nor need for mind or will of God in the mechanical model of the world. Newton's successors, for the most part, have sidestepped the origin of the world as an insoluble problem, but they came to be very certain as to its end in the universal stagnation of the "heat death". They could not figure out where the starry universe came from, but they satisfied themselves as to where it was going.

A simple statement of the shift that has come in the fundamental concept of the nature of the physical world is this: the discoveries in astronomy and the modern conception of the nature of the atoms makes the picture of the material universe as a running down machine as obsolete as the pre-Copernican system of astronomy. The modern view presents the world as a continuing evolutionary process, not to be interpreted in static terms of being but in dynamic terms of becoming. The final reality that science discovers is the infinite rhythm of cosmic energy that alternately creates and destroys the atoms and the stars.

It is by no means self-evident that this modern conception offers any more evidence of meaning and purpose in the universe than does the older picture of the running down machine. Belief that there is a moral order that inheres in the order of the world finds no firmer basis in the new than was to be found in the old world-view of science. Such a belief can stem only from a non-scientific, but not unscientific, postulate of the existence of God from whose nature flow moral and spiritual values and whose Will finds expression in the order of Nature.

But to conceive of God as pure spirit existing separate and apart from the world of the atoms leaves an unbridged gap between any will and purpose that may exist in the Divine mind and its expression in the march of either physical or historic events. To bridge that gap in our attempt at a synthesis of the religious and the scientific, we must think of Nature and God, not as two separate existences, but as two aspects of a single final reality that includes both the natural and the divine.

We have to make this same sort of a synthesis in our conception of man, "the unknown". Biologically he is an animal. Much of his behavior springs from those natural instinctive drives that are common to animals in general. But mysteriously coupled with these elements of purely animal origin are those constructive creative urges that transcend the animal and put the stamp of divinity upon the human spirit. Man has within himself the measure of his universe. In him are fused the blind energy of the atoms and the creative mind of God. Science and religion are two roads along which in the process of his spiritual evolution man approaches an ever fuller realization of himself.

In our present attempt to find a rational basis for Christian faith we shall look at the origin and growth of Christianity as a natural process in human evolution. We shall also try to see the development of the conceptual background of science as leading to a scientific description of nature and of natural law that will allow the possibility of an unfolding moral purpose in the order of nature and in human history.

Finally, we shall maintain that both science and religion arise from the necessity imposed on man, a physico-spiritual being, to adapt himself to a total physico-spiritual environment. Only in man's ability to adapt himself to this total environment can the human species demonstrate its fitness to survive.

CHAPTER 2

The Common Origin of Science and Religion

"Science and Religion are from a single source."

THOMAS AQUINAS

THERE IS NOTHING either novel or unique in the impulsion of the modern mind to unify the external and the inner elements of conscious experience. It is simply a renewal, under the conditions produced by the amazing growth of scientific knowledge, of the age-old struggle of man, a self-conscious being, to relate himself to the world of physical events. He feels himself to be an integral part of this world and at the same time something wholly separate and apart from it.

In the naive mind of the child or the primitive mind of the savage, there is probably no consciousness of self apart from objects of sense experience. The dual aspect of cognition is not present in animal consciousness. For the child of nature, the sun and the wind and the stars are a part of himself and he in turn is a part of them.

As in the growing child, so in the evolution of the human race there comes an awareness of the self as separate from that which is not self. The recognition of this cleavage calls into play two primal responses—fear and curiosity. The little child may first show fear of a strange new toy, but his curiosity soon overcomes his fears. He feels an innate urge to *know* all about the thing he fears. Here we see the scientific impulse in its most elemental form. Primitive man, in his dawning awareness of himself as something apart from nature, sees and fears her unfriendly aspects as hostile to himself. That fear arouses his aggressiveness toward his natural environment. Out of this there grows both a will to master and a will to placate the hostile powers he fears. In this ambivalent attitude are to be found the beginnings of both the scientific and the religious attitudes of primitive man to the world around him. Mingled with his fear and his aggressiveness is an insistent urge to *understand* this outer world that both threatens and preserves his life. Understanding involves a certain measure of identification of himself with the outer world. He recognizes his helplessness in the presence of the vast forces of nature, as well as his dependence upon their more friendly elements. The first step toward understanding is to ascribe personal qualities to them. For primitive man, nature in its unfriendly aspects appears as the expression of malignant powers bent on his destruction. He recognizes also its friendly manifestations and personifies these as beneficent deities, whose favors are secured by acts designed to appease their wrath. Having arrived at a consciousness of himself as something apart from nature, he effects a reunion by personifying those aspects of nature over which he has no control, and these personifications become objects of worship and veneration.

The fact of his own self-consciousness and his recognition of his dependence on nature make him a religious animal. The expression of the religious impulse has an important survival value. Religious rites are essentially social. Ceremonial is of necessity a community affair. The tribe, the unit of primitive life, is held together by totemic beliefs and practices. The totem, the tribal animal, is eaten in ritualistic celebrations by all the members of the tribe. It becomes the symbol of tribal unity. Religious beliefs and practices increase the capacity of the members of the tribe to act together for common ends, the securing of food, protection against wild beasts, and the inroads of hostile tribes.

Human society thus has its beginnings in religion. Individual and tribal activities, the planting and gathering of crops, the crises of life, birth, adolescence, mating, sickness and death, each has its own ritual in which meaningless rites and acts of practical insight are strangely combined. The functions of priest and magician are combined in one individual. The invoking of benevolent powers of nature and the placating of evil powers are united with primitive intelligence in the communal practices that are the expressions of religion in the savage state. Thus primitive religion has its origin in man's sense of his separation from nature. Its psychological drive is an inner urge to bridge that gap of isolation. Its growth is promoted by the practical necessities of tribal life.

The tremendous gap between the religion of primitive people and that of Western civilization is spanned by the intellectual and cultural development of the three great peoples of antiquity, the Greeks, the Romans and the Jews, the spiritual antecedents of the modern Western world.

Among the Greeks, we find the practice of magic and nature rites giving way to established forms of ritualistic worship. Gradually the shadowy outlines of the nature gods take on human form and assume human qualities. Folk lore becomes myth, usually connected with some traditional hero who is deified in the legendary accounts of his heroic exploits. The shadowy deities and demons of the savage become less and less personifications of nature, and more and more the expressions of racial and national traits, gods and goddesses who in their celestial abodes behave very much like their human creators. They are actuated by human passions, love, hate, jealousy. They and their heavenly affairs become the subjects of the poet's and the artist's play of fancy. The wizard and the magic worker of the primitive become a priestly craft ordained to the interpretation of the will of the gods. Priestcraft comes to exert a powerful influence over the lives and actions of the people. The content of religious belief becomes a mixture of myth, legend, tradition and poetic creation. Religious observances persist as the vestiges of seasonal festivals and primitive magic. At this stage mystery cults arise, groups whose members are initiated by secret rites, and who, by these ceremonials, are supposed to receive special gifts from the patron deity of the cult.

Gradually with increasing culture, naive faith gives place to scepticism among the educated classes. Philosophical speculation rationalizes the popular beliefs for the sophisticated, while traditional religious practices under the tutelage of the priests are incorporated into the social life of the common people. This latter is the stage which religion had reached among the Greeks and had been transmitted to their Roman conquerors at the beginning of the Christian era.

The history of the Jewish religion appears in somewhat different pattern. In the Old Testament we have a record of the evolution from primitive to formalized religion among the nomadic Semitic tribes of the Sinai peninsula that resulted in the monotheism of the Jew and the Mohammedan. Christianity is grafted upon the ancient Hebrew stock. Gradually, primitive polytheism was replaced by the worship of a single tribal deity. The Jahveh of the Israelites, whose earliest worship centered in the Ark of the Covenant and the Tabernacle, appears first as a protective deity, who takes the part of his chosen people against their tribal enemies. He is represented as a "jealous God" who punishes his people for any defection from their allegiance to his worship. The Mosaic law prescribed in minute detail not only the ceremonial of religious worship, but also laid down a multitude of regulations covering the practices of daily life. This law is purported to have been transmitted directly to Moses from the hand of Jahveh.

With the establishment as a nation of the Israelitish tribes in the narrow strip of land between the Jordan and the Mediterranean. the tent or tabernacle of Jahveh was replaced by the temple at Jerusalem. Throughout the troubled history of the Jewish people, the temple and temple worship remained the center of both the religious and the political life of the nation. Meanwhile, the original Mosaic ritual was added to by vast accretions of traditional prescriptions that came in time to comprise a ceremonial that included almost every act of the Jew's daily life. On the other hand, the primitive conception of Jahveh, the tribal god, was expanded and refined by the teachings and writings of the prophets into the broader conception of one true God who demanded of his people not only the observance of the ceremonial law but also imposed commands of righteousness, justice and mercy. Thus while Judaism centered around the idea of a single spiritual deity, yet religion for the Jew became largely a matter of strict observance of ceremonial rites and ethical conduct both handed down from God through the mediation of priests and prophets. The conception of God as the creator was overshadowed by that of God, the righteous law-giver.

Religion and religious observances were of primary importance in the life of the individual and of the nation. In Hebrew prophesy and poetry we find some of the most exalted expressions of man's religious and ethical aspirations. These sacred writings form the ancient scripture of two of the great monotheistic religions of the world. The Ten Commandments are the basis of the moral and legal codes of Western civilization.

Such in broad outline is a naturalistic account of the evolution from their primitive sources of the religion of the ancient Greeks and of the Jews. With the Greeks, the culmination of this movement was a developed philosophy which centuries later came to form the metaphysical background for both modern science and Christian theology. At the dawn of the Christian era, Judaism had arrived at the conception of a personal God and had established a highly elaborated form of worship and an ethical religion.

As has been suggested, curiosity is the primal expression of the scientific impulse. The unknown has terrors which only knowledge can dispel. The scientific urge has also an element of the aggressive that is so characteristic of the human animal. The scientific impulse arises from an instinctive will to *know* and no less from an innate will to power. In their earliest stages, both science and religion are motivated by an inner necessity to control the environment. These two diverse elements in magic were the beginnings of science and religion. Both arise from the inherent qualities of human psychology, and both have survival value for the human species.

In its earliest expression, the scientific impulse is directed to practical ends. It had its origin when man first began to observe and record the invariable sequences of natural events and to utilize this knowledge in his struggle for subsistence and shelter. Experimental science arose in his first crude attempts to devise mechanical means of securing desired results. Even the observation of the heavens in the first instance served practical purposes. Twenty centuries before Christ, the astrologers of the Euphrates valley had obtained fairly accurate knowledge of the movements and periods of the heavenly bodies. This knowledge the priestcraft made the basis of an elaborate system of astrology, from which the course of future events might supposedly be predicted. Thus in its origin science like religion was mingled with superstition and magic. Primitive science was a mixture of observed facts, legend and superstition. The flight of birds, the periodic recurrence of the seasons, the rise and fall of the rivers, drouths, floods and storms, all were ascribed to the will of supernatural beings, but through the superior *scientific* knowledge of the priests, the observed facts were utilized for enhancing the power of the priestcraft, and at the same time they furthered primitive man's efforts to provide food and shelter.

Science as knowledge divorced from religion and magic arose when ancient man began to make measurements. The idea and methods of making measurements of time, distance and weight arose in the civilizations of Babylon and Egypt that antedated the Christian era by twenty-five centuries.

The scientific knowledge that originated in these earlier civilizations was transmitted for the most part to the Western world by way of the intermediate culture of the Greeks. The tiny peninsula of the Greek homeland was at the crossroads of travel between the East and the West. Greek travelers and traders found their way to all parts of the civilized world that bordered the Mediterranean. Thus the science, philosophy and religions that had developed through centuries in the valleys of the Euphrates and the Nile were transplanted to the fertile soil of the receptive, creative minds of the classical Greeks. There they were transformed into the highly developed systems of thought that centuries later were appropriated by modern science and Christian theology.

Greek thinkers were, for the most part, more concerned with the rational than with the empirical. They drew their facts largely from alien sources. Their chief concern was to fit these facts into logical systems of thought. Hence their science was largely deductive, based on preconceived notions of the nature of the world. Their role was that of the middleman of ideas, who appropriated the scientific lore of the great civilizations of the past, wrapped it up in neat metaphysical packages, to be delivered centuries later to the rising civilization of the West. Medieval science and theology accepted without scrutiny these packages on the basis of their labelled contents and the prestige of their origin. The break between science and the Church came when Galileo insisted upon examining the contents of the package labelled "Mechanics" and discarded them as useless in a science based on facts discovered and verified by observation and experiment.

Although Greek science was based more on philosophic speculations than empirical knowledge, nevertheless foreshadowings of the fundamental concepts of modern science are to be found in Greek metaphysics. In the accounts which the philosophers of antiquity gave of the reality that is assumed to lie back of the world of physical phenomena, we find the origin of those differences in fundamental ideas that have existed all through the history of philosophy and science. The modern materialistic concept of the atomic structure of the world is to be found in the teachings of Democritus and the ancient atomists. More than four hundred years before Christ they taught that the physical properties of material bodies are only the interpretations that our senses give to movements and combinations of ultimate particles, the atoms. These differ "in size and shape, but are identical in substance". Besides the atoms there is nothing. Their movements are strictly determined by antecedent causes, "nothing happens without cause". Here we have the basic concept of atomistic mechanism, which, until very recent times, was the theoretical foundation of modern physics and chemistry.

At the other end of the ideological spectrum from atomic materialism is the attitude of mind shown by Pythagoras and his followers. For them the underlying reality was mental and was to be discovered by the deductive processes of mathematics. No doubt the land surveyors of Babylon and Egypt had long since stumbled on to the fact of the relation between the three sides of a right triangle, but to Pythagoras is ascribed the honor of its mathematical demonstration. With the Pythagoreans, mathematics and mysticism were joined. The harmony of certain musical intervals was ascribed to the simple ratios of the numerical lengths of strings and air columns that produced these intervals. From this was taken the wild leap that the secret of the universe is to be found in the magic of numbers. Some one has said that even a bad theory is more useful than no theory at all. The truth of this may find illustration in the fact that twenty centuries after Pythagoras, Kepler the mathematician was moved to make his monumental study of planetary motion by the mystical and scientifically mistaken ideas of Pythagoras. However, if the shade of Pythagoras could know the tremendous difference that modern scientists find between Uranium 238 and Uranium 235, he might flatter himself that his ideas of the magic properties of numbers was not so far wrong after all.

But the speculations of these earlier Greek philosophers who exhibited the scientific trend of thought were eclipsed by the metaphysical systems developed by Plato and Aristotle. While the teachings of their master Socrates had a greater impact upon the men of his time, so much so that he was put to death as a propounder of subversive doctrines, yet it was through the writings of his two great disciples that the Socratic spirit of critical analysis of ideas became a part of the intellectual heritage of Western civilization.

It is beyond our present purpose and certainly beyond the ability of the writer even to summarize the systems of philosophy that bear the names of Plato and Aristotle. We are concerned only to see how the two streams of thought whose origins are to be found in their writings can be traced in the history of ideas that have dominated both modern science and Christian teachings.

The Platonic mind sees the ultimate reality of the world as absolute ideas, eternally and unchangeably existent in the mind of God. The world of sense experience is but the play of transient shadows of these eternal realities upon the walls of human consciousness. The truth about the world lies in the relationships between these ideas and can only be attained by the processes of mathematical reasoning. This conception is the background of mathematical physics. For example, the reality back of all electromagnetic phenomena is assumed to be in the relations that are symbolically expressed in the equations of the electromagnetic field. Going far beyond this, Einstein has put all the facts of both electromagnetism and gravitation into the neat single package that contains only the mathematical relations of the General Theory of Relativity. The terrifying secret of atomic energy is revealed in the now familiar equation $E=mc^2$ which is the latest testimony of modern science to the validity of the Platonian approach to reality.

On the religious side, we find in Christian thought all through the ages the influence of the Platonic conception of the real existence of ideas. In fact, the heart of all Christian teaching regarding the nature of the Christ is to be found in what the theologians call the "Logos Doctrine". This is set forth in explicit terms in the first verse of the Gospel of Saint John: "In the beginning was the Word (Idea) and the Word was with God and the Word was God." Platonism is deeply implanted in the thought and concepts of both modern science and Christian dogma.

Even more wide spread and deeply seated in both Western science and religion are the ideas of Aristotle. His encyclopedic mind collected and systematized the knowledge and the ideas of the ancient world that had crystallized in Greek thought. The son of a physician, he accepted and probably used in some degree observational and experimental methods of arriving at facts in the fields of physiology and medicine. In physics and cosmology however, he joined Plato in rejecting experiment in favor of speculation based on current notions of the nature of the physical world. What medieval thinkers accepted as coming from Aristotle, Aristotle had in turn accepted from earlier philosophers regarding the fundamental concepts of time, space and matter. These became current notions regarding the fundamental physical concepts at the time of the rise of modern science two thousand years after Aristotle. Thus it was that, while Galileo refused to accept as verified truth the classical teachings as to the behavior of material bodies under the action of mechanical forces, yet his ideas as to the ultimate nature of time, space and motion were still those of the master mind of ancient Greece.

It is worth noting that the cleavage between Aristotelian and Newtonian mechanics lies in their treatment of the relationship between force and the motion of a material body. Aristotle taught that a continuous motion could result only from the continuing action of a moving force. The continuing motion of the heavenly bodies thus called for the uninterrupted operation of an efficient cause of motion. The final cause of all motion is the "Unmoved Mover", the metaphysical God of Aristotle's philosophy. In Newtonian mechanics no continuing force is required to maintain motion. Newton's First Law of Motion states that a body in motion will remain in motion. Inertia is the fundamental property of matter. Thus the pious Christian, Sir Isaac Newton, had no need in his mechanics for the metaphysical God of the pagan Greek Aristotle. Nevertheless, Newton, and following him the whole body of thought in modern physics up to the time of Einstein, rested on the Aristotelian postulate of the independent existence of space and time. In his Theory of Relativity Einstein resolved the contradictions that were inherent in the Aristotelian concepts, thus scoring a triumph for Platonism in the conflict of ideas that arose in ancient Athens twenty-four centuries ago.

This same conflict between what may be called the idealistic and the naturalistic attitudes of mind can be discerned throughout the history of Christian doctrine. Up until the beginning of the fourteenth century the conflict between the Platonic and Aristotelian interpretation of the Christian tradition was waged within the councils of the Church. After the tenth century when translations into Latin of the writings of the Greek masters first became available to Catholic scholars, the struggle as to which of the two philosophies should be the official orthodoxy of the Church was waged furiously in the universities and between the various monastic orders. It was in the first half of the thirteenth century that Thomas Aquinas, a Dominican monk, set forth in a monumental work his "Summa Theologiae", a theology that integrated Greek philosophy, the teaching of Scripture and of the Fathers of the Christian tradition into a single self-consistent body of thought. In this work, it was Aristotle rather than

Plato whose thought occupied first place in this synthesis and, since the Church has put the official seal of orthodoxy on Thomasian philosophy, Catholic dogma is in a very real sense Aristotelian. As a modern Catholic scholar, Jacques Maritain, has put it, "Saint Thomas baptized Aristotle".

This masterpiece of medieval scholarship had two far reaching results that together have profoundly affected both the religious and scientific development of the Western world. On the one hand it gave to the historic Church a theology that, granting its initial premises, is *logically* impregnable. On the other, it so identified the religious and the scientific that the authority of the Church was extended to cover the whole field of intellectual endeavor. The criterion of scientific truth was agreement with the teachings of Aristotle as interpreted by the supreme authority of the Church. It was Galileo's failure to meet this criterion in his scientific teachings that brought him before the Inquisition and caused his works to be banned as damnable heresy.

The real impact of Greek metaphysics was in its influence on the intellectual outlook of the rising culture of the West centuries after the "glory that was Greece" had faded from the human scene. It is a significant fact that it had little influence on the contemporary popular religion nor did it give any immediate impetus to the progress of science. It was almost a century later in the Greek colonies in the south of Italy and in Egypt that the scientific spirit of the Greeks found expression in the geometry of Euclid and the physical discoveries of Archimedes. Among the Athenians, it created an attitude of sophisticated scepticism in the minds of the educated regarding the traditional gods which the common people continued to worship. These latter satisfied the religious needs of the imaginative temper of the masses for whom the speculations of the philosophers were a sealed book. For their contemporaries Plato and Aristotle spoke in an unknown tongue. It was for the philosophers of the Middle Ages, confronted with the supreme mystery that is at the heart of Christianity, that the language of Greek metaphysics had worth and meaning.

Plato and Aristotle mark the high point in Greek philosophic thought. With the conquests of Alexander, first of the Peloponnesian states and then of the whole of eastern Asia, came the beginning of that "time of trouble" for Hellenic civilization, the end of which was the absorption of this center of ancient culture in the vast empire of Rome. Alexander's conquests opened the gates of the hitherto isolated and self-contained Greek state to a flood of alien influences from eastern Asia. This fact, together with loss of national independence and political prestige, initiated among the Greeks that "schism of the soul", which Arnold Toynbee finds to be characteristic of a disintegrating civilization. Such a schism results in the loss of creative faculty in the great personalities of a society and the acceptance by the intellectual minority of some sort of a philosophy of escape. It finds expression among the uneducated masses in the infiltration of the foreign elements into religious practices and the admission of alien gods into the circle of deities of popular worship.

It was during this period of the evergrowing power of the Roman Empire and the decline of intellectual interests and artistic taste that the escape philosophies of Epicureanism and Stoicism came to occupy a commanding place in the nobler minds of the times. This period marks also the introduction and acceptance by a large segment of the populace of mystery cults of eastern origin. During the later portion of the period, emperor worship was decreed and established as the official religion throughout the Empire as a means of unifying the widely diverse elements of the far flung Roman rule. As we contemplate the spiritually chaotic state of the world in the centuries that covered the greatness and decline of ancient Rome, it is all too easy to draw the deadly parallel with this our hour of scientific and material greatness and religious bewilderment.

Then, faith in old gods was dying. A great age was moving to its close, and in its decline common men lost that sense of security and well-being that only an ordered society can create. Nobler souls withdrew into a philosophy of detachment and stoical acceptance of the will of Fate. Humbler men drifted aimlessly or sought salvation in the emotional excesses of alien cults.

This was the "dark night of the souls" of men that came before the rising of the new Star over Bethlehem. In a later chapter we shall return to the events that attended its rising. But first we shall want to look at the revolutionary shift in man's outlook on the material universe and to trace the evolution of ideas and concepts of the nature of the world that came with the onward march of modern science.

We shall find in the history of the amazing growth of science during the last three and one half centuries a definite pattern in the evolution of scientific ideas and concepts. From the starting point of experimentally established facts, theories have been devised to reduce these facts to a rational order. With the ever increasing store of facts, contradictions appear that call for modifications in existing theories and revision of the concepts on which they are based. We shall trace this pattern of growth from the purely mechanistic world view of seventeenth century physics, which offered no account of the origin of life and mind and afforded no basis for belief in the possibility of purpose in the meaningless *dance* of the atoms, to that of the twentieth century that sees placed in human hands the god-like power either for destruction or creation that lies in the *energy* of the atoms.

Having followed this pattern of development in the various branches of science, we shall return in our final chapter to the interpretation in terms of human evolution of the origin and meaning of historic Christianity. In such a synthesis the Christian believer may find assurance that his faith is not in vain, and the devout man of science may see the religious motivation of his scientific quest of truth.

Chapter 3

The World as a Machine

"In truth there are only Atoms and a Void."

DEMOCRITUS

"Nothing happens without cause, but with a cause and of necessity." LEUCIPPUS

THEOLOGICAL AND METAPHYSICAL SPECULATION were the major preoccupations of the great minds of the long period that stretched from the decline and final collapse of Graeco-Roman civilization through the intellectual and political chaos of the Dark Ages to the revival of learning that came with the Renaissance. It is true that there was some scientific progress. The history of science records the achievements of Archimedes, the first and greatest of the physicists of the ancient world to conform to the modern ideal, and of Euclid, with his development of geometry. At Alexandria, a Greek colony, advancement was recorded in medicine, geography and astronomy. Ptolemy gave to the world a comprehensive treatise on astronomy and trigonometry and a theory of the heavenly bodies which was to persist until the time of Copernicus and Kepler. Here too, alchemy, the forerunner of chemistry, had its origin. Roman contributions to science were largely practical in the field of geography and engineering.

There was little in the way of broad scientific advancement during the early centuries of the Christian era. The infusion of Christian faith, with its background of Hebraic theology, into the welter of pagan ritual, mystery cults and Neo-Platonic mysticism resulted in a world-view in both learned and popular thought that precluded any serious interest in the problem of material reality. Gradually, as the decaying political power of the Roman Empire was succeeded by the spiritual and temporal power of the Church, these diverse elements were fused by scholastic dialectic into a unified, though scarcely coherent, body of theological philosophic dogma comprised, as Dampier-Whetham has put it, "of astrology, alchemy, magic and theosophy . . . in which the medieval mind felt at home." Incorporated into this body of teaching was the acceptance of the authority of the Scriptures as interpreted by the Church, and with it much of Plato's metaphysics and the logic and scientific outlook of Aristotle. It was not until the thirteenth century that the diverse elements in medieval thought were synthesized into a self-consistent, logical body of doctrine by Thomas Aquinas, the greatest of medieval theologians.

With the revival of learning and under the stimulus of the geographical discoveries of the fifteenth century, thinkers both in and out of the Church began to turn their attention increasingly to the investigation of natural phenomena. Observation and experiment rather than philosophical and theological dogma came to be recognized as the paths to knowledge of the material world. The study of things as they are, rather than as authority thought they ought to be, was the starting point for the work of the leaders of thought. Moreover, the whole intellectual and spiritual outlook of the Western World was undergoing a profound change. It was as if a spark from the ancient flame of the free spirit of the Greeks had kindled a new fire in the hearts and minds of the virile semi-barbarous hordes that had overwhelmed the decadent power of Rome and were becoming the new nations of western Europe. The young and vigorous mind of the Renaissance no longer felt "at home" in a world of theological dogma prescribed by ecclesiastical tradition. The lure of the unknown in external nature once more began to exert its spell on the human spirit, and men turned from the contemplation of the God of theology to the quest of objective truth in the operation of natural processes. A series of great names stand out like milestones on this long and painful road that the mind had to travel from the medieval to the modern view. The works of Roger Bacon, Leonardo, Copernicus, Gilbert of Colchester, Harvey, Kepler and Galileo mark the initial steps of the progress from scholasticism to modern science.

It is to Galileo that history gives the title of father of modern physical science—but his work would have been barren as a root in dry ground had it not been supplemented by that of a score of men of genius whose scientific achievements make the seventeenth century an outstanding epoch in the history of human thought. Descartes, Pascal, Huygens, Boyle, Newton and Leibnitz are the names which are associated with the beginning of the modern movement in physics, chemistry and mathematics. To these must be added a host of lesser names, who, following the trail of quantitative experiment blazed by Galileo, cleared the way for the triumphal progress of science in succeeding centuries. The transition from the medieval to the modern world-view was a process of slow evolution rather than an abrupt break in the continuity of the intellectual life of the times. In religion the Reformation came as the culmination of a long period of ferment that had been going on within the Church itself. In the mind of Copernicus, the chief argument in favor of shifting the center of the universe from the earth to the sun was the fact that this shift resulted in greater mathematical simplicity in accounting for the movements of the heavenly bodies. In this he reverted to the ancient Greek view that the world must be constituted in accordance with our ideas of mathematical harmony. To an even greater degree, Kepler's labor in the mathematical deduction of the laws of planetary motion was inspired by the belief that God had created the solar system according to the Pythagorean conception of the harmony of numbers. Copernicus and Kepler were in this regard both very ancient and at the same time very modern in their attitude of mind. Thus the foundation upon which Newton was to build his great generalization of the universal laws of mechanics was laid largely by minds which were essentially cast more in the scholastic than in the scientific mold.

Many volumes have been written setting forth the multitude of causes that conspired to produce that tremendous upsurge of the human spirit, the Renaissance. Far below the surface of men's lives, buried beneath the weight of ecclesiasticism and traditional authority, lay the germ of all true science—the scriptural injunction, "Prove all things. Hold fast to that which is good." Slowly the assurance given in Jesus' teaching, "Ye shall know the truth, and the truth shall make you free," was taking root in the minds of men. When Galileo, standing before the tribunal of the Inquisition, declared, "It is not in the power of any creature to make anything to be true or false or otherwise than of their own nature and in fact they are," he was but giving voice to a truth, the seeds of which had been planted in the human mind by the founder of the Christian faith.

The hiatus of more than sixteen centuries was but the period of germination of the seed of freedom of thought and devotion to truth whose flowering and fruit are the vast achievements of modern science. It is well to remember how great was the lump of ignorance, superstition, false ideas and bigotry in which the leaven of Jesus' ideal of spiritual values was hidden. It is well to note too that the rapid march of science followed close upon the freeing of men's thought from the power of tradition that came with the religious revolt of the Reformation.

With Galileo began the revolution in thought and method which in the short span of three centuries has completely transformed our views of the material world and has given us a mastery over our physical environment that the medieval mind could not have dreamed of. Isaac Newton was born the year after Galileo died. Upon the foundation of Galileo's experimentally verified mechanics, Newton built a framework of mathematical generalization which has carried the whole fabric of modern physical science. The fundamental concepts of Newtonian mechanics were not new. They are to be found in the speculations of Aristotle and Democritus. Matter exists in and of itself, independently of mind. The sequence of physical events occurs under strict laws of mechanical causation. Time, space and matter are independent and final realities. Motion is definable in terms of time and space. Matter is inert, and any portion of matter is of itself incapable of any change in its own movement which is not accompanied by an equal opposite change in the movements of some other portion of matter. Force is that which produces a change in the motion of matter. All we know about matter mechanically is that it requires a force to produce a change in its motion, and force is measured by the time rate at which it produces a change of motion. Fortunately for the advancement of science, Newton was not balked by the logical difficulty involved in giving independent definitions to his two fundamental concepts of mass and force. Otherwise he would have found himself blocked as were the ancient Greek logicians who proved conclusively that logically motion is impossible. Newton took the concept of *force* as something immediately given by experience and hence beyond definition. As a matter of fact, as Bridgman and others have pointed out, our idea of force arises from the muscular sensation experienced when we try to change the motion of material bodies—a sensation which entirely lacks the numerical properties with which it becomes endowed in Newton's classical laws of motion. What Newton did is beautifully typical of the scientific procedure of abstracting from sense experience those elements which are expressible in quantitative terms and of building with these abstractions an image world of mathematical relationships.

It is no part of our present purpose to undertake a critical analysis of the conceptual basis of Newtonian mechanics.

Much has been written since Einstein, and even before him, on this subject. All that is intended is to bring into sharp focus the limits within which the conclusions reached by classical physics are valid in view of the fundamental concepts and postulates, both expressed and implicit, upon which its findings are based. Since physical and chemical concepts and methods have been carried into modern biology and psychology far beyond the limits originally imposed, it is well to have clearly in mind the boundaries beyond which the concept of mechanism is not applicable.

Newtonian mechanics rests on idealized concepts of time, space, matter and force as measurable quantities. Time and space are absolute in the sense that they cannot be reduced to simpler concepts. Time is that which is measured (reduced to numbers) by periodically recurring physical events—the rotation of the earth, the swinging of a pendulum. Space is that which is reduced to number by measuring rods. As Newton conceived it space had only geometrical properties. Matter and force are mutually related by the experimentally determined facts of accelerated motion. Since the only influence which can be exerted on any portion of matter must at the same time act upon other matter in the opposite sense, and since the change of motion produced in a unit time is the measure of the force that produces it, it follows that within a closed system no increase or decrease of the total amount of motion of all the bodies comprising the system can occur—the classical law of the conservation of momentum.

Newton conceived of material bodies as individual and separate from each other save as they affect each other by gravitational or other mechanical forces. Each individual object is an aggregate of smaller particles held together by their mutual attraction. These internal forces are not essentially different in character from the forces which produce the acceleration of relative motion between two bodies. Thus to Democritus' idea of the universe as constituted of "atoms and a void," Newton added the concept of forces acting through space between the atoms. A universe so conceived is completely determined if we postulate the universality of the laws of force and motion, for the configuration and motions of all the atoms at any moment of time is causally dependent upon their configuration and motion at the preceding moment. Hence any future state is implicit in the present state, since all that can happen in the interim between present and future is a succession of conditions each of which is the necessary consequence of conditions existing in the preceding moment of time. Mechanistic determinism is therefore inherent in the fundamental concepts and postulates of Newtonian mechanics. By his definition of matter and force Newton precluded the possibility of any portion of matter being subject to any influence other than the force which arises from the existence of other matter. Since the universe is composed of particles, each of which is inert, that is to say incapable of instituting motion in and of itself, then the sum total of all the atoms must be inert in the sense that motions cannot arise that are not inherent in those motions which already exist.

Thus Newtonian mechanics is built upon a framework of pure abstractions, from which, by definition, all causes save mechanical ones are excluded. Newton did not concern himself with the question of the origin and nature of matter and motion, nor did he attempt any solution of the problem of their relation to mind. He was concerned only to express the observed behavior of matter in terms of mathematical relationships so general that they would include all the observed phenomena. The fall of the traditional apple, the rotation of the moon about the earth, the relation of the periods of rotation of the planets to their respective distances from the sun as given by Kepler's laws, are all deducible by mathematical reasoning from the universal law of gravitational attraction. Essentially what Newton did was to start with the raw material of sense experience and to fashion from it an "image world" of mathematical relationships.

The validity of the process rests upon the degree to which the sequence of events in the image world corresponds to that occurring in the world of sense experience.

Now this "image world," since its conceptual content is mathematical, is in a sense a product of the mind and hence satisfies the mind's necessity for understanding. But unlike the speculative world of Greek thought, it starts with sense experience and finds its justification in its correspondence with the same experience.

Galileo's experimental verification of the elementary facts of mechanics and Newton's synthesis of these facts into a comprehensive mathematical scheme marked the beginning of the creation of the image world of science which has been the outstanding achievement of the modern mind.

In this day of the supremacy of science we are apt to fail to recognize the limitations of scientific knowledge, and to limit all truth to so-called "scientific truth". For a clear-cut statement of the limitations that physical science has imposed upon itself, we cannot do better than to quote von Helmholtz, the greatest scientific mind which Germany produced in the nineteenth century.

In 1847 in a paper dealing with the equivalence of mechanical energy, heat and electric processes, he stated: "Science regards the phenomena of the exterior world according to two processes of abstraction: in the first place, it looks upon them as simple existences, without regard to their action upon our organs of sense or upon each other—in this aspect they are named *matter*. The existence of matter in itself is to us something tranquil and devoid of action; in it we distinguish merely the relation of space and mass, which is assumed to be eternally unchangeable. Matter in itself can therefore partake of one change only—a change which has reference to space, that is, motion. Natural objects are not, however, thus passive; in fact, we come to a knowledge of their existence solely from their actions upon our organs of sense and infer from these actions a something which acts.

When, therefore, we wish to make actual application of our idea of matter, we can only do it by means of a second abstraction, and ascribe to it properties which in the first case were excluded from our idea, namely the capability of producing effects. It is evident that in the application of the ideas of matter and force to nature, the two forms should never be separated; a mass of pure matter would, as far as we and nature are concerned, be a nullity inasmuch as no action could be wrought by it either upon our organs of sense or upon the remaining portion of nature. A pure force would be something which must have a basis, and yet which has no basis; for the basis we name matter. It would be just as erroneous to define matter as something which has an actual existence and force as an idea which has no corresponding reality. Both on the contrary are abstractions from the actual formed in precisely similar ways. Matter is only discernible by its forces and not by itself."[1]

Elsewhere he states: "The final aim of theoretic natural science is therefore to discover the ultimate and unchangeable causes of natural phenomena. Whether all the processes of nature be actually referrible to such—whether changes occur which are not subject to the laws of necessary causation, but spring from spontaneity or freedom, this is not the place to decide. It is at all events clear that the science whose object is to comprehend nature must proceed from the assumption that it is comprehensible and in accordance with this assumption investigate and conclude, until perhaps, she (science) is at length admonished by irrefragable facts that there are limits beyond which she cannot proceed."[2]

This beautifully lucid statement sets in sharp relief both the essence of the purely scientific attitude toward all physical phenomena and also the limitation which this attitude imposes upon all scientific knowledge. Matter in and of itself is a pure abstraction—"something tranquil and de-

[1] von Helmholtz (tr. by John Tyndall) *Source Book of Physics*, p. 213, McGraw-Hill, 1935.

[2] Ibid.

void of action," which can only penetrate the world of conscious experience by virtue of its possession of that other pure abstraction, "the capability of producing effects, of exerting force."

This capability of producing effects, that is changes in matter, finally emerged as the physical concept *energy*. Gradually during the first two centuries after Newton this concept was clarified and the universal fact of the conservation of energy in all physical changes was established. Accordingly matter and energy came to be recognized as comprising the whole content of the physical universe.

Meanwhile, chemical science had proceeded toward the establishment of that other implication of the Newtonian view of matter, namely its atomic character. Newton ascribed chemical properties and chemical changes to the action of forces between the ultimate microscopic particles of which material bodies are composed, forces not essentially different from the force of gravitation between gross material bodies. Gradually as alchemy developed into chemistry, the older vague notions of chemical processes as due to the transfer of imponderable fluids gave place to the modern view of chemical changes as being due to regroupings of the atoms of which all substances are composed.

Thus the commonest of chemical changes, combustion, was originally conceived of as the release from a burning substance of an imponderable "phlogiston." In 1784 Priestley heated the "red calx of mercury," collected the gas given off, and discovered its unusual power to support combustion and its necessity for the respiration of animals. He described it as "dephlogisticated air." A few years later Lavoisier, with the aid of the balance, did for chemistry what Galileo two centuries earlier had done for mechanics, and by the same sort of scientific procedure — the abandonment of purely qualitative experimentation for exact measurement. Modern chemistry may be said to have its rise in Lavoisier's demonstration of the conservation of mass in the classic experiment which is the introduction of the college freshman of today to experimental chemistry, namely, that the combined masses of the products of combustion are equal to the sum of the masses of what is burned and the oxygen used in the burning. Numerous experiments of a similar nature yielded the same general results, that the amount of matter as measured by the balance is neither increased nor diminished by any change, either physical or chemical, which it may undergo. As a result chemistry, hitherto a somewhat nebulous collection of qualitative knowledge of the properties and behavior of substances, joined with physics in becoming an exact science in the sense that every chemical change may be symbolized by a stoichiometric equation based on the fundamental law of the conservation of matter. Lavoisier was sent to the guillotine by the masters of the French Revolution in 1794, but not until after he had published his *Elementary Treatise on Chemistry*, a book which produced as great a revolution in the field of chemistry as Galileo and Newton had effected in physics.

Almost contemporaneous with the work of Lavoisier was that of Proust, Richter and Gay-Lussac establishing the fundamental facts of chemical combinations. Upon these facts Dalton at the beginning of the nineteenth century proposed the atomic theory upon which the whole body of modern chemistry rests. Dalton asserted that "all bodies of sensible magnitude, whether liquid or solid, are constituted of a vast number of extremely small particles or atoms bound together by a force of attraction. Chemical analysis and synthesis can go no farther than to the separation of particles one from another and to their reunion. No new creation or destruction of matter is within the reach of chemical agency. We might as well attempt to introduce a new planet into the solar system or to annihilate one already in existence as to create or destroy a particle of hydrogen."[3] Further, he states

[3] John Dalton in *A History of Science*, Dampier-Whetham, Cambridge University Press, 1929.

that the atoms of each element all have the same weight, and the relative weights of the atoms of different elements are to be inferred from the proportions in which these elements are found in compound substances.

While many refinements and modifications of the theory as originally proposed by Dalton have been made in the development of modern chemistry, yet the fundamental picture of the material universe as made up of atomic particles of a limited number of kinds, between which forces of attraction and repulsion act, has formed the background of all chemical experiment and speculation. Thus the fundamental concepts of chemistry have been those of Newtonian mechanics reduced to the submicroscopic scale of atomic dimensions. Up until the recent discoveries of subatomic physics, the essential difference between the atoms of the various elements was considered to be the difference in their atomic weights—a numerical property, neat, compact and intellectually satisfying. With the development of each new method of research, new elements have been discovered and the number of known elements has increased from the twenty of Dalton's time to more than ninety. Moreover, the importance attached to the atomic weights of the elements has not been misplaced, for it has been found that there is a definite relation between the chemical properties of the elements and their atomic weights.

If the chemical elements be arranged in the order of their atomic weights, certain chemical properties are found to recur periodically in the series as we go from the lighter to the heavier elements. Thus numbers 2, 10 and 18 in the series are the chemically similar inert gases, helium, neon and argon, respectively. Numbers 3, 11 and 19 are the alkali metals, lithium, sodium and potassium. The Russian chemist Mendeleeff summarized these and a multitude of similar correspondences in what is known as the Periodic Law in chemistry, a generalization which has been of tremendous value both in stimulating the search for hitherto undiscovered elements to fill the gaps in the periodic table and in suggesting the idea of a common basis for all the elements —an idea which has found full confirmation in the twentieth-century development of subatomic physics.

The essential correctness of the atomic theory as a working basis for chemical research has been amply proven by the achievements of modern chemistry. Though the chemical atom is far too small to be directly perceived by any of our senses, yet our whole industrial civilization is based upon the postulate of its objective reality.

During the first half of the nineteenth century the concept of energy was expanded to include *heat*, the kinetic energy of the random motions of molecules of solids, liquids and gases, and also to include the capacity to produce change that resides in electric currents. During this period the mutual convertibility of these various forms of energy was established, and the numerical conversion factors were experimentally determined. In 1843 Joule showed that 772 foot-pounds of mechanical energy are equivalent to the heat required to raise the temperature of one pound of water one degree Fahrenheit. Helmholtz showed that if account be taken of the heat generated and the mechanical work done then the total quantity of energy expended in an electrical circuit is equal to the chemical or mechanical work done in generating the current flowing in that circuit.

Meanwhile, partial identification of the forces operating in chemical changes with the forces exerted upon each other by electrically charged bodies had been made. The experiments of Faraday and Davy had established the fact that the transfer of chemically equivalent weights of different elements is effected by the passage of equal quantities of electricity through electrolytic solutions, thus suggesting the atomic nature of electricity as well as of matter.

These facts are all comprised in two generalized statements, recognized to be universally true—the law of the conservation of matter and the law of the conservation of energy. Since in every change that takes place the total quantity of matter and also the total quantity of energy is unaltered, it follows that the material and energy content of the universe has remained and must forever remain unchanged. Hence in the midst of infinite change we have two unchangeable constants—matter and energy.

During the first half of the 19th century physical science came to recognize a second universal fact with regard to energy transfers and transformations in nature. The statement of this fact goes under the formidable name of the "Second Law of Thermodynamics." The enunciation and clarification of this law as it applies to the physics of heat and mechanical energy is to be credited to Carnot, Clausius and Kelvin. Later Willard Gibbs, one of the greatest scientific minds that America has produced, carried the ideas and principles developed in the theory of heat engines into the field of chemistry, thus integrating the relatively new sciences of physical chemistry and electrochemistry with the older mechanics.

The first thermodynamic law is that of the conservation of energy. The second refers to the "dissipation of energy," and is a generalized statement of the universally observed fact that when energy is either transferred from one body to another, or is changed from one to another of its various forms, there is always a toll exacted that reduces the available energy that results from the transfer. By "available energy" is meant energy that, under the given conditions, is capable of producing further change.

A familiar illustration of the law is the fact that the mechanical efficiency of a machine, the ratio of the useful work that can be got out of it to that which is put into it, is always less than unity. The difference between the input and output energies appears as the heat developed by friction in the bearings. There is no destruction or loss of energy, but the energy that is dissipated as heat is not available for producing mechanical effects. This amounts to saying that without a supply of energy from some external source any machine, no matter how nearly perfect, must exhaust its initial supply of energy and in the course of time run down.

In order to formulate mathematically this universal fact of the loss of availability in energy transfers, Clausius developed a new concept to which he gave the pleasant-sounding name "entropy." This concept can only be stated in mathematical terms, but it is so defined that *decrease in available energy* due to energy transfers in any closed system of bodies is measured by the *increase of entropy* of the system. The second law of thermodynamics, therefore, is ordinarily spoken of as the "law of increasing entropy" and is simply stated by saying that any change that can occur in an isolated material system increases the entropy of the system.

Obviously the concept of entropy cannot be applied to just one material particle. The idea applies only to the over-all thermodynamic behavior of vast numbers of particles. Theoretically the motion and position of each particle is determined by the forces that arise from the presence and motion of all other particles. This has been shown to be the same as it would be if the motion of every particle were a matter of pure chance. It follows therefore that in any assembly of atoms the over-all state which the group as a whole will in time attain is the *most probable* state as determined by the mathematical laws of chance. The difference in entropy between two states as determined by thermodynamic measurements is thus proportional to the difference in the probabilities of the two states as computed from statistical laws based on the conception of pure chance. The law of increasing entropy simply says that those transfers of energy that occur of themselves in nature take place in such a way as to increase the probability of the final over that of the initial condition. In other words, according to the second law, "Time Marches On," and "on" is in the direction of increasing entropy toward future conditions that, according to the laws of chance, are more probable than are those of the present.

Water runs down hill, heat flows from hot bodies to cold bodies, the carbon of coal combines with the oxygen of air to produce carbon dioxide and generate heat. All these are examples of the "downhill process," changes that, once started, continue until a more probable state is reached, one of mechanical, thermal or chemical equilibrium. The most probable distribution of energy among a very large number of particles is that in which each particle gives energy to and receives energy from all the other particles in equal amounts. Therefore it is one in which the probability of any further change in the system as a whole is zero. This state in known as *thermodynamic equilibrium.*

As will have been noted, this law of increasing entropy is based on observed facts and the assumption that the only properties of material particles are those assumed in Newtonian mechanics. Any prediction based on this law, of a future condition within a closed system is, therefore, a matter of probability rather than of absolute certainty. Thus, a gallon of water at 200 degrees, mixed with an equal quantity at 100 degrees, will yield two gallons of water at 150 degrees. The total quantity of heat energy in the mixture is the same as that of the original components. Conceivably it should be possible to go back to the original condition by a separation of the rapidly moving molecules of the hot water from the more slowly moving molecules of the cold. But thermodynamic considerations show that an increase of entropy results from the mixing process. Hence the probability of a reversal of the process is so small that we say it is impossible. Heat energy will of itself pass from a hot body to a colder one, but a flow from cold to hot never occurs without an over-compensatory flow in the opposite direction somewhere else. It is for this reason that we have to supply electric power to our refrigerators. We have to pay for the improbable state of a region maintained at a lower temperature than its surroundings.

Carrying this principle to its logical conclusion, nineteenth century physics arrived at the conception of a material world progressing to a final state of thermodynamic equilibrium, a state in which nothing further can happen. According to this view the vast stores of energy concentrated in the sun and the stars are being radiated into cold space. That portion of it which reaches the earth may serve to reverse temporarily the downhill tendency here, as in the photosynthesis of highly organized molecules in plants. This, however, is but an eddy in the downstream tendency of things in general.

From the initial impulse given by the method of quantitative experiment as a means of acquiring reliable data and the application of mathematical processes to the correlation of these data, physical science in the course of two hundred years arrived at a unified view of a material world governed by precisely formulated mathematical laws. This view conceived of the universe as composed of a fixed and unalterable number of discrete atoms. These atoms are of a limited number of kinds, having different chemical properties which are in some way associated with numerical magnitudes, the atomic weights. The atoms are composed of an abstraction called *matter*, defined in the first instance in terms of another abstraction, *force*. In the evolution of scientific thought the capability of matter of exerting *force* on other matter was clarified into the concept of *energy*, a physical entity, which is conserved in all material changes. In this view, all that occurs in this ever-changing world can be reduced by analysis to regrouping and movements in space of the atoms with accompanying transfers of energy from one group to another. So conceived, man's physical environment presents the aspects of a vast mechanism in which the only and ultimate realities are atoms and energy. The energy of the universe must be assumed to have been originally distributed unevenly among the atoms, resulting in a state of unstable equilibrium. From this unstable, highly improbable initial state, under the operation of the second law of thermodynamics, energy would be transferred from the more highly energized to the less highly energized atoms. This process, carried on indefinitely, leads finally to that most probable state of complete thermodynamic equilibrium. In this state the total energy of the universe is conserved, but none is available for producing further change. Thus the ultimate fate of the physical universe as a matter of unescapable scientific deduction is the so-called "heat death" of which physical science has had so much to say.

As a mere matter of hard common sense, the only thing a mechanism can do without an external source of power is to "run down," and since by the mechanistic hypothesis there is nothing external to the material universe, it is not surprising that mechanistic science should predict for it the fate of universal stagnation.

However we may feel about this conclusion that must follow from the hypothesis of atomistic mechanism, it must be said that the practical achievements of an objective approach to the problem of material reality has within a period of three centuries completely transformed the external conditions of civilized life. The changes that have resulted from the application of science to the mastery of man's physical environment are greater than all that are recorded since the beginning of history up to the seventeenth century. As Arthur Compton has put it: "Our life today differs from our grandfathers' more than did theirs from the life of 2000 years before." Science and the scientific method produced a tremendous acceleration in the rate of man's material progress. Twenty centuries lie between Archimedes, the last physical scientist of the ancient world, and Galileo, the first of the moderns. But scarcely more than a century after Galileo the invention of the steam engine marked the beginning of the age of steam. Another century and the age of electricity had begun. For twenty-five centuries the atomic theory of Democritus remained sterile as purely philosophical speculation. Within a century and a half after its modern version was announced by Dalton, it has borne fruit in industrial and commercial applications that affect every phase of civilized life.

These are the practical results of the scientific approach and of scientific methods as applied to the material world. It is upon the basis of these practical achievements that science has come to speak with an almost final authority to the mind of our day. Whatever one may think of atomistic mechanism as a complete philosophy, it must be admitted that as a working hypothesis it has had the superlative merit of yielding results. But even more, because of the degree to which it satisfies the human intellect, must we grant validity within its field to this scientific view of reality. Atomistic mechanism creates an image world, unified, mathematically compact, and practically useful in the control of natural forces. Physical happenings are tied together in mathematically formulated laws that give to the sequences in nature the aspect of logical necessity.

But the satisfaction of this intellectual need leaves still deeper needs of the human spirit unsatisfied. Man's spirit does not live on intellectual bread alone. Moreover, as a scientific theory atomistic mechanism leaves out one-half of the world of objective fact. To conceive of all natural processes as flowing out of the redistribution of energy among inert atoms excludes the possibility of the reverse process of evolution that biological science invokes in explanation of the order of organic nature. A purely mechanistic philosophy ignores the facts of biological evolution, leaving the origin of life and the emergence of mind as extra-physical happenings outside the realm of physical description. If all reality be reduced to a process involving only a transfer of physical energy, then consciousness becomes a mysterious byproduct of the chemistry of the brain. The mind itself assumes the role of passive observer of a vast cosmic machine engaged in the meaningless process of running down. At the same time its activity is in some unexplainable way an expression of that process. The idea of freedom and purpose in either man or nature is sheer illusion derived from a deceptive feeling in consciousness. Human behavior becomes the necessary response of a collection of atoms, the human body, to blind physical forces originating in a world that happens to be in a state of unstable thermodynamic equilibrium.

The attitude of mind that such a philosophy engenders (perhaps one could put it the other way around and say the type of mind that created such a philosophy) can not be better expressed than in the words of the great modern mathematician and logician, Bertrand Russell, when he said, "The whole temple of man's achievement must inevitably be buried beneath the debris of a universe in ruins—this if not quite beyond dispute is yet so nearly certain that no philosophy which rejects it can hope to stand."[4]

It may be remarked that the particular "temple of man's achievement" known as Western Civilization stands in far more imminent danger of destruction at man's own hands than from the universal ruin which the logical mind of Mr. Russell foresees. But it is nonetheless true that the pessimistic fatalism induced by a mechanistic philosophy has permeated the thinking of today and is responsible in no small degree for the "thinning and wavering" of religious faith in the lives of many thoughtful people. The intellectual satisfaction afforded by atomistic mechanism has been purchased at the price of an increased sense of isolation and impotence of man as a conscious spiritual being in a world of dead matter and impersonal energy.

Mechanism leaves us with three uncorrelated unknowns: (a) God, or some other unidentified agency to which is to be

[4] Thomas Mosher, *A Free Man's Worship*, Portland, Maine, 1923.

ascribed the "wound-up" state from which the universe is running down, (b) *life,* whose origin and evolution defy explanation in purely mechanistic terms, and (c) that unique something which each man designates as "I," the individual conscious self, the substratum of all experience that exists outside the categories of matter and energy. A mechanistic philosophy effects no unification of these three aspects of the world of human experience with the world of atoms and energy that it postulates.

In this situation we have the choice of two obvious alternatives. The first is that the idea of God and of the existence of creative purpose in either man or nature is only a superstition or false belief that scientific knowledge has not yet been able to eradicate from human thought. The second has already been suggested—that the scientific view is only a partial view that apprehends merely those aspects of reality that are essentially quantitative, and therefore leaves all questions of moral and spiritual values and religious beliefs to nonscientific fields of thought. This latter is, for the most part, the attitude of the greatest scientific minds from Newton down. They have recognized that a mechanically ordered world is an "image world," a pure construct of the mind created for a specific end. Newton himself, a man of deeply religious temper, ascribed the order that his genius had discovered in the material universe to the operation of a Divine Mind that ordained the natural laws which govern its movements. Shortly before his death he said, "I have kept an eye upon such principles as might work with considering men for the belief of a Deity, and nothing can rejoice me more than to find them useful for that purpose." For him the physical universe was a machine, created by God and controlled by divinely ordained laws. As already noted, Helmholtz placed the whole question of whether there are effects which do not spring from physico-chemical causes as outside the domain of physical science.

For the predominantly scientific mind this segregation

of the world of science from the world of spiritual values is not particularly disturbing. There are enough unsolved problems in science itself to keep the man of science from bothering very much about a problem that after all is something for the philosophers to worry about. But the failure of mechanism to account for vital phenomena, and to include the evolutionary process in its conceptual framework of the totality of nature, calls for an extension of our ideas of external reality beyond the self-imposed limits of mechanistic theory. Moreover, if we assume that there is an element in man's nature other than the purely material, then we may quite rationally maintain that there is also a spiritual element in the natural world from which he has evolved and which sustains his life in both its physical and spiritual aspects.

We turn in our next chapter to a consideration of a possible correlation of the two processes, the downhill process of increasing entropy and the creative process of evolution, both of which must be included in a comprehensive scientific account of the external world.

CHAPTER 4

Life in a Running-Down World

"Evolution begins with amorphous living matter—and ends in thinking Man endowed with a conscience."

LE COMTE DU NOUY[1]

"I certainly believe that the world is running down. It means that our epoch illustrates one special type of order. That does not mean that there are not some other types of order of which you and I have not the faintest notion, unless perchance they are to be found in our highest mentality, and are unperceived by us in their true relevance to the future."

ALFRED NORTH WHITEHEAD[2]

PHYSICAL SCIENTISTS HAVE GENERALLY recognized that matter and energy do not compass the whole of reality. Their quest has not been for an all-embracing philosophy in which all experience is to be comprehended. Only in very recent years has physics found itself in any way concerned with metaphysics. Matter is material—mind is mental, and, frankly admitting the dualism of an outer and an inner world of experience and ignoring the question of the relation between the two, physical science has concentrated upon the relation between phenomena that presumably exist in an outer world. Only one assumption is made, namely, that ultimately the natural order is a rational order, and that reason guided by experiment and observation can discover that order in what is apparent chaos.

Physical science has left to philosophy the problem of the relation between mind and matter. As we have seen, it

[1] *Human Destiny.* Longmans, Green & Co., 1947.

[2] *Essays in Science and Philosophy.* Philosophical Library, New York, 1947.

is tacitly assumed throughout all physical theory, and often explicitly stated, that nowhere is the chain of physical causation broken to admit of any effective action of a nonphysical agent. This obviously limits physical science to the field of inert matter, that is to say, matter that is active only as it serves as a vehicle for energy received from and imparted to other matter. This naturally suggests the question as to whether there is any matter that is not inert. The obvious answer is in the affirmative—living matter is not inert and therefore living matter is not included in the world of atomistic mechanism. This immediately makes a line of cleavage dividing the external world into the lifeless and the living, or, since life is always expressed in organisms, into the inorganic and the organic.

Do physical and chemical laws apply to the behavior of organisms? If they do, wherein lies the essential difference between the living and the lifeless? Is it a necessary conclusion that the living as well as the inanimate part of creation is mechanically determined? If these material laws do *not* apply to living matter, then what is the nature of the forces that operate in the organic world and are not effective in inert matter? These are the questions which for the past two centuries have divided biological scientists into the two opposed camps of mechanists and vitalists. According to the mechanist's view the processes that take place in living organisms are in no essential different from those which take place in the chemical and physical laboratory. Life is a series of chemical and physical reactions, tremendously complicated to be sure, but all theoretically explicable in terms that are used by the physical scientist in dealing with inanimate matter. Failure thus to explain vital processes, say the mechanists, results from our incomplete knowledge of all the physical factors involved rather than from the presence of ultra-physical causes that operate on living matter. The vitalist, on the other hand, maintains that in the living organism effective influences are operative which must, by their very nature, escape detection and measurement by purely physical means.

Now vast quantities of good black ink and many reams of fair white paper have been used in the controversy that has been waged for generations between the exponents of the two views. The essentials of the controversy are to be found long before the seventeenth century rise of mechanism. The Greek atomists maintained that the soul consists of fine round smooth atoms, like those of fire, which were diffused among the grosser atoms of the body—a theory which suggests the very modern one of the existence of free electrons among the atoms of electrical conductors, which electrons account for the electrical conductivity of metals.

Plato, on the other hand, maintained the incorporeal nature of the animating force and is said to have expressed the wish that all of the works of Democritus, the first of the atomists, might be burned.

Throughout the entire history of modern biology the conflict has gone on. Thanks to the triumphs of mechanism in the fields of physics and chemistry, the odds have come to favor more and more the mechanistic view on the part of biologists in general, but always with a minority who have insisted upon the existence of extra-physical forces that operate exclusively in the living organism. Biophysics and biochemistry are the most intensively worked fields of biological research. It is not surprising that this should be the case, for the experimental method can be employed successfully only where, theoretically at least, both cause and effect belong in the same category. Physical methods cannot be employed in the study of nonphysical causes of vital phenomena. Even the philosophical vitalist becomes a practical mechanist when he goes into the biological laboratory to obtain data to support his vitalistic conceptions of the life processes. Likewise the mechanist would be hard put to account for the peculiar arrangement of the material objects which constitute the experimental equipment in the biologist's laboratory. Even more difficulty would be encountered in an attempt to explain in terms of mechanistic determinism the sequence of physical events which are his own activities as he conducts his scientific investigations. Certainly he cannot evoke any law of mechanical causation to account for the peculiar behavior of that particular organism, the scientist himself, as he goes about his quest of truth along the road of experiment. He assumes that here, at least, conscious purpose is operative as an effective cause in the chain of physical events.

Thus the paradox: as a practical scientist the *vitalist* proceeds upon a working basis of mechanism, and the *mechanist* must think of his own activities as something more than a series of automatic responses to external stimuli. By and large, the controversy seems to resolve itself into a question of the relative emphasis placed upon the inner and the outer aspects of experience. As a conscious being each of us is aware of a sense of power to exercise voluntary control over the movements of that portion of matter which constitutes his own body. I can stretch out my arm and hold it there, even though as a mere matter of mechanics a lifeless arm would under the force of gravity fall to the side. Projecting this subjective experience into the apparently purposive activities that mark the life process in other organisms, I am led to the acceptance of the vitalistic postulate that living matter is in some unexplainable way subject to nonmaterial influences which effectively control its movements.

On the other hand, if I take a more objective view of myself as an organism, and consider all of those processes that, quite independently of conscious volition, conspire to maintain my body as an integrated whole, I am inclined to accept the mechanistic interpretation. The action of the heart is mechanically that of a pump which maintains a constant circulation of the blood through the arteries, veins and capillaries. The lungs operate as bellows on the simplest of mechanical principles. The processes of respiration, digestion and excretion are chemical processes nearly all of which can be duplicated outside any organism. The impulses that are propagated along the nerves are electrical in their nature. And finally, the energy needed to produce all those movements that we call vital processes is supplied by the food that is eaten and transformed into those movements by chemical, electrical and mechanical changes, not essentially different from those by which the chemical energy of gasoline is converted into the kinetic energy of a ton of steel moving sixty miles an hour. Viewed externally in this way, life seems to be an integral part of the mechanistic picture.

As to the question which of these two descriptions of the living organism is true, the answer must be that both are true in so far as they are useful. As with matter, so with life—its essence must always elude our complete understanding. We can only know it in terms of its relationships.

If we externalize life and deal with it objectively, then life will present its mechanistic aspect. The organism will appear as a bafflingly intricate mechanism, part of a mechanistic cosmos from which it receives energy and to which it returns that energy according to physical and chemical laws. If, however, we seek to know life from the immediate experience of being alive, then our description must be in terms that do not appear in the glossary of physics and chemistry. We recognize it as dynamic and creative, imposing form and order upon matter, responding to its material environment and in turn modifying that environment to its own ends.

The great generalization of nineteenth-century biology was the doctrine of evolution. In the breadth of its scope and in the unification it has effected in biological science, it is comparable with the laws of conservation of matter and energy in the physical sciences. Like all the great generalizations of modern science, it has its foreshadowing in some of the speculations of the Greeks, and there are certain premonitory flashes of it in the philosophers of the seventeenth and eighteenth centuries. But the honor of marshalling the vast multitude of facts in the animal and vegetable kingdoms, upon which the doctrine is based, properly belongs to Charles Darwin and Alfred Russell Wallace, who almost simultaneously presented the theory of evolution as an explanation of the origin of living species.

The storm of controversy that arose following the publication in 1859 of Darwin's *The Origin of Species* was a modern version of the encounter between Galileo and the Inquisition. Darwin's account was in direct conflict with a literal interpretation of the Biblical account of the creation and was bitterly attacked by the theologians of his day.

The conflict was waged on essentially the same ground, only the issue in the later struggle was between the findings of science and the authority of the Scripture rather than of the Church. Orthodoxy taught that the world and its living inhabitants were created *de novo* by Deity and that Man, the crowning act of that creation, was made in the image of God himself. Darwin taught that the "web of life" weaves itself through the whole of the animate world and that the creation which Genesis ascribes to "the beginning" is a continuing process. Each part of nature is vitally connected, either intimately or remotely, with every other part. Nothing lives unto itself. Life appears as a universal drive in matter, ever seeking new forms of expression in minute variations from established patterns, preserving its creatures by marvelous adaptations to adverse environments, ruthlessly sifting out its ill-adapted children in the struggle of existence. In Darwin's view man as an organism appears not as a separate creation but as a part of nature, the contemporary stage of one line in the evolution of the vast kingdom of the vertebrates. If man bears the stamp of his Creator, it is in his spiritual essence, and not in his anatomical structure. In the latter he bears too many close family resemblances to his not very distant cousins, the anthropoid apes, for him successfully to deny the relationship.

Here again is that duality that results from viewing

the same set of facts in their inner and outer aspects. As an organism present-day man appears as the species *sapiens* (a somewhat flattering descriptive term, perhaps) of the genus *homo*, a branch of the order of primates, phylogenetically related to the orang and the gorilla. Experienced from within, against the background of his own consciousness, coupled with an awareness of an ever expanding world of outer reality, man sees himself as something unique and different from all the rest of animate nature.

The evolutionary view of life has done much more than give a rational account of the origin of the countless forms that comprise the world of living beings. It presents all life from the simplest unicellular organism to the most highly evolved species as a continuous chain of biological events. It connects the plant and animal life of the present with extinct species of past geological periods and finds recorded in the living organism of today the history of its inheritance extending far back into the ages when the physical environment was far different from what it is now.

The unit of life is the cell, with its unique properties of retaining its form and function while continuously changing its substance by taking from its environment those elements of which it is composed. Chemically the life process is essentially the same throughout the whole of nature from the simple single celled organism such as the algae, or the amoeba, where it is little more than a sustained chemical reaction between the protoplasm of the cell and its watery environment, up through the ever increasing diversification of the higher orders of living beings. In all matter that is alive, be it the segmented body of the worm, the petals of a flower, or the brain of Albert Einstein, the living substance of the constituent cells is the same protoplasm that someone poetically, if not scientifically, described as a "handful of dust which God enchants."

Biochemistry may be defined as the chemistry of protoplasm, and biophysics as the physics of protoplasm.

Biologists tell us that protoplasm is not a true chemical compound in the sense that its composition is quantitatively constant. It contains all the chemical elements usually found in organic compounds, carbon, hydrogen, oxygen and nitrogen, together with both organic and inorganic salts and water in large amounts—some 85 or 90 per cent.

Now living protoplasm, although it is not a true compound, has the unique property of maintaining its composition practically constant while taking part in a chemical change or a whole series of chemical changes. In the inorganic world chemical changes affect all the factors in chemical reactions. When coal (carbon) is burned (oxidized) the carbon ceases to be carbon as such but is found in the gaseous carbon dioxide, the product of combustion. Chemical energy is liberated as heat. The reaction ceases when all the carbon is oxidized. Essentially the same chemical process supplies the energy of a living organism, the amoeba, let us say. But there is this essential difference, that in the case of the amoeba the energy supplied is used in part to extract more oxidizable material, i.e., food from the environment, so that while the body of the animal is the scene of a continuous chemical reaction and is itself taking part in that reaction, its chemical composition remains practically unchanged. Looking at the chemistry of the life process, the living organism appears as a device through which the available chemical energy of food is converted into heat and movement. The heat is utilized to maintain a temperature at which the chemical process will continue, while the movement serves in part the purpose of securing more food, to supply more energy, and so on in an endless cycle. It is as if we had a self-stoking furnace made of combustible material which is all the time burning, but in so doing supplies energy to operate the stoker that constantly replaces the matter which is burned. The living being is constantly changing but never wholly changed.

We may, if we like, put this obviously oversimplified

picture of the life process into a somewhat formidable verbal statement by quoting F.S.C. Northrup's definition of a living thing as a "temporary dynamic heterogeneous equilibrium between internal and external physicochemical materials."[3] When we have defined the terms used in this definition we shall find that we have essentially what has just been pictured as going on in that tiny speck of nucleated jelly which we all met in our elementary course in biology, the amoeba. He lives to get food and he gets food in order to live. It is worth noting in passing how this idea of purpose enters inevitably into our account of vital processes. Coal burns, iron rusts, dead tissue decays. These are simply statements of fact bearing no implication as to any purpose which is served thereby. But when we speak of essentially these same chemical processes, the taking up of oxygen by the blood stream in respiration, and the transfer of oxygen through the circulatory system to the living cells where, in the process of oxidation, it supplies the energy that is needed to maintain *life,* we imply a purposive element in the sequence of events. Description involves more than the mere physics and chemistry of what goes on. That purpose is the maintenance of life of the organism.

We may accordingly describe the individual physical and chemical changes that take place between a living organism and its material environment in physico-chemical terms, but we will have missed the peculiarly characteristic quality of life itself if we omit the fact of the interrelatedness of these individual activities by which this "dynamic equilibrium" tends to perpetuate itself in the life process. This interrelatedness has meaning only as purpose, an end to be achieved, namely, the preservation of the organism. Proceeding by the process of scientific analysis, all that we can hope to discover about life is this series of physicochemical changes and their relations to each other. In so doing we have abstracted from vital phenomena those nu-

[3] *Science and First Principles,* Macmillan, New York, 1931.

merical aspects with which the intellect can deal, and we discover only a physico-chemical mechanism. The unique distinctive quality of life escapes us, simply because the only terms in which we can describe it are not included in the categories of objective science.

Biological science finds that the physics and chemistry of organic processes follow the laws of the conservation of matter and of energy. The material intake and outgo of the animal body exactly balance each other, just as they did in Lavoisier's experiment. Similarly, quantitative experiments have shown that the measured energy output of the human body, taking account of the heat generated and the mechanical work done, is, within the limits of experimental error, equal to the free energy content of the food eaten. So far as these two general laws of behavior of inert matter are concerned, the living organism may be considered as a localized series of physico-chemical reactions.

It is when we look at vital processes in conjunction with the law of increasing entropy that we begin to question the complete scientific validity of the mechanistic interpretation of organic life. In the first place, the mechanical efficiency of the organism as a machine is considerably greater than the efficiency of a heat engine working through vastly greater temperature range. This means that in some way life has found a means of circumventing locally and temporarily at least the general downhill tendency of inanimate nature. The living organism dissipates less available energy as heat doing a given amount of work than does a cyclically operating heat engine. In the second place, the life process shows itself not wholly governed by the operation of the second law of thermodynamics. It is only in the living organism that we find in nature any exception to the operation of that law in the equalization of temperatures between hot and cold bodies. The body of a warm-blooded animal is maintained at a constant temperature regardless of the temperature of its surroundings. A lifeless body comes in time to assume the temperature of its immediate environment either by a flow of heat to the body, if it is colder, or from the body, if it is warmer than bodies around it. Now it is quite beside the point to argue that this end result can be achieved by purely mechanical means, as for example, in the design of the cooling system of an automobile engine. When the automotive engineer devises a method whereby a motor is maintained at a temperature that will insure its successful operation under a wide range of external temperatures, he is accomplishing by obviously mechanical means the same thing that is achieved automatically by the nicely adjusted series of internal reactions in the body of the vertebrate that keeps its temperature continuously the same regardless of winter's cold or summer's heat. Both are means of locally circumventing the normal operation of the second law of thermodynamics, just as the design of an aerofoil is a means of preventing the aviator from paying the penalty of violating the law of gravity.

It is equally irrelevant to urge, in favor of the mechanistic interpretation, the fact that each step of the intricate series of internal reactions by which the body temperature is kept constant is explainable in physico-chemical terms. It would be quite as logical to argue the absence of purpose in the cooling system of the motor car by pointing out that all the individual movements by which the end results are obtained are the necessary results of purely mechanical laws.

Examples might be multiplied indefinitely to emphasize the fact that the distinguishing characteristic of an organism as opposed to a mechanism is the coordination of purely physical and chemical reactions in such a way as to maintain the dynamic equilibrium between the organism and the environment. For example, consider the human body as an internal combustion engine. The energy is supplied by the chemical process of oxidation of the food. This oxidation takes place in the protoplasm of the individual cells. The necessary oxygen is taken from the air by the blood stream in the lungs. At the same time the blood gives up the carbon dioxide which is the exhaust gas residue from the oxidation in the tissues. Thus on its way *to* the lungs the blood serves as a carrier of the waste product, carbon dioxide, while the outgoing stream carries the essential oxygen to the body cells. It is as if in our engine one conduit served both as the air intake and at the same time as the exhaust pipe. This looks as though nature had gone at least one better than the engineer until we are told that, as a mere matter of chemistry, the oxidation of the haemoglobin, the oxygen-carrying constituent of the blood, reduces the amount of carbon dioxide that can be taken up by the blood, and vice versa, the external presence of carbon dioxide causes the haemoglobin to give up a large proportion of its oxygen. Thus the apparently anomalous fact that in the lungs the blood stream takes up oxygen and gives up carbon dioxide, while in the cells the action is just the reverse, turns out to be a mere matter of physical chemistry and not a special device which nature uses only in vital processes.

This two-way operation of the blood stream in carrying oxygen to the tissues, and the products of oxidation away from the tissues, results from a unique property of that interesting substance, haemoglobin. It is a highly organized molecule consisting of a protein combined with a complex acid group containing iron. It combines with oxygen to form an unstable oxide, thus increasing the oxygen-carrying capacity of the blood stream. This property of haemoglobin serves the same purpose as is served by a forced draft under the boilers of a power plant, i.e., speeds up the process of oxidation.

Haemoglobin holds in loose chemical combination a large quantity of oxygen. The degree of dissociation of this compound of oxygen and haemoglobin is determined by a number of factors in such a way as to make it particularly well adapted to the purpose it serves. First, the amount of oxide formed increases with the pressure of the oxygen but reaches a maximum at the partial pressure of the oxygen in the lungs, approximately 160 millimeters of mercury. Further, the presence of carbon dioxide or other acid or salt lowers the oxygen-holding power. If an inventor seeking for some means whereby oxygen could be taken from the air and distributed to the individual cells of an organism, and the carbon dioxide removed, had invented haemoglobin, he would have been entitled to a basic patent, and possibly a Nobel prize. Nowhere else in either nature or the chemical laboratory do we find any substance with the properties required to do just this thing.

In the lungs, where the oxygen pressure is high and the carbon dioxide pressure is low, the haemoglobin becomes chemically saturated with oxygen. In the tissues of the body, due to the presence of salts and carbon dioxide, nascent oxygen is set free, which, combining with the oxidizable constituents of the cells, supplies heat and muscular energy. But when the haemoglobin has given up a large part of its oxygen, another particularly useful property appears, namely, its increased capacity for uniting with carbon dioxide. The life of the cell requires that the carbon dioxide formed in the oxidation be removed. (The secret of Carrel's success in maintaining animal tissue alive for an indefinite time independently of any organism was in his discovery of an artificial means of removing the toxic waste products of the life process.) The arterial blood, freed of its oxygen, is now ready to take up the carbon dioxide and carry it back to the lungs, where, due to the high pressure of the atmospheric oxygen, a process occurs which is just the reverse of that which takes place in the cells. Due to the combination of the physical and chemical properties of haemoglobin, the blood stream acts as a sort of continuous bucket brigade. The molecules of haemoglobin serve as the buckets. In the lungs they empty their load of carbon dioxide replacing it with oxygen. In the tissues they give up oxygen and take on carbon dioxide.

Now it is to be noted that this series of events forms an unbroken chain of causally connected physico-chemical changes. At no point do we have to postulate the existence of any extra-physical agencies. Given the physical and chemical properties of haemoglobin plus the conditions existing in the atmosphere and in the living animal, the oxygenation of the blood in the lungs and the oxidation of cell material in the cells follow as a matter of physical necessity. But—and here comes the distinctive property of life—the hypothesis of pure mechanism fails completely to explain how all the conditions are maintained that must be maintained in order for these physico-chemical changes to occur in a continuously operating cycle. Looking at the matter from the mechanistic point of view we should expect that the nice adjustment between the three variables, oxygen, haemoglobin and carbon dioxide could be maintained only under constant external conditions of atmospheric pressure, temperature and the like. As a matter of experience, we find that wide variations may occur in the external phase, and that these variations are accompanied by variation in the internal phase whereby the dynamic equilibrium is maintained. Moreover it appears that other factors, such as the alkalinity of the blood stream as measured by the hydrogen ion concentration and the salinity due to the presence of sodium, potassium, calcium and magnesium salts are involved. Variations in any one of these involve variations in all the others.

One of the most surprising examples of this compensatory coordination is to be noted in the fact that while a large number of variable factors can individually affect the alkalinity of the blood stream, yet the net result of wide individual variations in these factors is practically nil in affecting the hydrogen ion concentration upon whose constancy the life of the organism depends. The "team work" between the various factors which affect this condition, so necessary for life, is far beyond description in any save purposive terms.

The work of L. J. Henderson and J. S. Haldane on the chemistry and physics of the blood gives a fascinating picture of perfect coordination of chemical changes by means of which the conditions necessary to the life of the organism are maintained constant even in the presence of wide variations in both the external and the internal factors of the dynamic equilibrium.

All through the organic world, these adaptations of purely physico-chemical means to vital ends appear. We have cited the chemistry of the blood as an example, particularly well worked out by physiologists, of the sort of thing that constantly rewards the scientific quest. Within the organism itself we find relatedness between the operations of the individual organs and the chemistry of their secretions. Externally we find the organism purposively adapting itself to environmental conditions. The growing by an animal of a heavy coat of fur in the fall and winter and the shedding of it in the spring may perhaps all be explained in physico-chemical terms, which only a physiologist would understand. In terms of purpose a child who puts on his overcoat in cold weather can understand it. The scientific search yields always the *how* in ever increasing degrees of complexities of physico-chemical reactions. Science discovers *design,* but the designer always eludes the analytic method. Biology adds another unknown, Life, to the physical and chemical unknowns of Matter and Energy.

In terms of matter and energy, physical science accounts for the events in an inanimate world on the basis of mechanical causation. In so doing it reveals the "downhill" tendency expressed in the second law of thermodynamics. Energy tends to distribute itself in matter in such a way as constantly to decrease the possibility of further changes. As a mechanism the material universe is "running down." "Time's arrow," to use Eddington's expression, points in the direction of increasing entropy toward the "heat death." Biological science, on the other hand, discloses a world in which the mechanically improbable is always taking place. Organization, the use of physical means in achieving vital ends, continuity of form and pattern in the midst of continuous change in material content, and evolution in time from the elemental to the complex, from the more probable single-celled organism to the highly evolved species with their complicated functional adaptations—this is the direction in which "time's arrow" points in the living world. Evolution finds causation in the *pull of the future.* Mechanism finds it only in the *drive of the past.* It is for this reason that we can always find explanation of the individual operations of life processes in physical terms. The purposive coordination of these processes for the maintenance of the life of the organism defies description in these terms.

Still more does mechanism leave us in the dark when we raise the question of the origin of life. It has long been a fundamental assumption, supported by a wealth of experiment, that "all life comes from the living." The notion of spontaneous generation has been considered by biologists as belonging in the same category as perpetual motion by the physicists. The unquestioning mind is quite content to accept the scriptural account, "In the beginning, God created the heavens and the earth" with all that is therein. But the scientific mind insists upon raising the question "How?" and "From what?" The doctrine of evolution makes the account of the origin of species by Divine fiat an allegorical summary of a creative process that, beginning in the far distant past of geological ages, continues up to the present moment. But evolution fails to account for the beginning of that process in what is generally conceived of as an otherwise lifeless world. Given the first living cell, evolution can trace something of the pattern of the web of life in its myriad forms up to genus *homo.* It can travel the road from amoeba to man. But over the road from the uninhabited air and earth and sea of the cooling planet, torn from the hot body of its ancestral sun by a celestial accident, to the appearance of those first miraculous bits of nucleated jelly, living cells, evolution so far has had to post the sign, "Not open for traffic."

Various theories of the origin of life have been proposed. There is the possibility suggested by many scientists that with the swarm of meteorites that continuously come within the reach of the earth's gravitational field, hardy organisms might have been brought from other planets. Experiments show that certain forms of life may pass through very great extremes of both heat and cold and still retain their vitality. Admitting this as a possibility, the problem of the initiation of the life cycle is simply pushed back into the unknown conditions of another planet. Its origin remains unsolved.

Another proposal is that the life principle is inherent in the fundamental chemical properties of the compounds of carbon, hydrogen, oxygen and nitrogen, and that given the proper conditions of temperature and humidity life emerges simply as a necessary result of those properties, just as water emerges as a necessary result of the chemical properties of the hydrogen and oxygen which compose it. In other words, presupposing the chemical elements of which protoplasm is composed, with their inherent chemical properties, and the cosmically unique conditions that exist on this earth, then matter will of itself originate the series of synthetic dynamic processes which, in time and through a process of evolution, result in the world of living beings.

This conception of the origin of life, while fairly satisfying from the evolutionary point of view, departs radically from the concepts of atomistic mechanism, with its necessary corollary of changes that can take place only in the direction of increasing entropy. Under this law the only emergents from the chemical properties of carbon, hydrogen and oxygen are carbon dioxide and water. Carbon and hydrogen burn (oxidize) and in so doing give up energy in the form of heat, random molecular motion, a process in line with the downhill tendency expressed in the second law of thermodynamics. The building up of atoms of these elements into the complex heavy molecules of the carbohydrates, starch and sugar, is in the opposite direction, and occurs in nature only in the living tissue of growing plants. Similarly, the uphill process of the formation of nitric acid (and thus nitrates) from hydrogen, nitrogen and oxygen is an uphill process occurring in nature only in the bodies of animals and as a result of the action of bacteria on certain plants.*

Evidently the explanation of the emergence of life as a necessary result of the chemical properties of its constituent elements is open to the logical difficulty that it explains the origin in terms of the results of life. It is like explaining the hen in terms of the egg, and then explaining the egg in terms of the hen. Moreover, if we ignore the logical difficulty, we have still to account for the concurrence of the chemical properties of the life elements, carbon, hydrogen, oxygen and nitrogen, that makes it possible to build them up into the very large molecular aggregates found in organic compounds and, at the same time, the peculiar fitness of the elements themselves and their simple compounds, water and carbon dioxide, both to maintain the environmental conditions necessary for life and to play the roles they play in the vital processes themselves. Accepting the theory of the chemically necessary emergence of life, we must either allow the idea of purpose in the cosmic scheme—looking to life as an end product—or we must ascribe to blind chance a concurrence of physical and chemical facts so improbable as to defy statement in mathematical terms.† The origin of life is the most improbable event that could possibly occur in a completely mechanical world.

* One should also add the well-known fact of the synthesis of nitric acid by powerful electric discharges.

† Dr. George H. Gallup, the well-known statistician, has said: "I could prove God statistically—the chance that all the functions of an individual would just happen is a statistical monstrosity."

While it appears that vital processes seem to run counter to the mechanistic trend from the less probable to the more probable atomic groupings and distributions of energy and, while mechanism fails to present any satisfactory account of the origin of life, it still has to be recognized that in the long run the downhill tendency wins out. Life's apparent victory over the law of increasing entropy is only temporary and local. Life comes from the living, but more than this life is maintained at the expense of other life. The elements found in the food of the animal are, to be sure, found in abundance in the air, earth and sea. But only as these elements are built into the complex molecules of organic compounds by the vital processes of plants or other animals do they possess the free energy which gives them food value. Nevertheless, the chemical end products of animal body chemistry are material from which this free energy is missing. What has not been converted into mechanical energy has been dissipated as heat, and the over-all result is an increase of entropy, the inexorable exaction imposed on all "becoming" by the second law of thermodynamics. In this sense the living organism is a mechanism whose operation reduces the free energy and increases the entropy of the universe.

We are told that the source of the energy of vital processes is the energy of sunlight, and that the uphill process required in the photosynthesis of complex organic molecules is accomplished by that wonder worker of all the chemical compounds found in nature, chlorophyll, the green pigment of the leaves of growing plants. In its chemical composition chlorophyll is closely related to that other of life's cleverest inventions, haemoglobin, which plays the leading role in the chemistry of animal metabolism. Magnesium in chlorophyll replaces the iron of haemoglobin. It is interesting to note that of these two closely related compounds one is essential to the life of plants, the other to the life of the warm-blooded animals.

Chlorophyll has the property of strongly absorbing

radiation in that region of the spectrum corresponding to the maximum energy of sunlight. This energy is apparently used in reducing carbon dioxide and, in the presence of water vapor, producing organic carbon compounds. Now this is an uphill process, since the available energy of the products of the reaction is greater than that of the original compounds. It may be represented thus:

$$xCO_2 + xH_2O + \underset{\text{(energy)}}{\text{Sunlight}} \nearrow C_x H_{2x} O_x + xO_2$$

The downhill reaction, which would occur in non-living compounds would be:

$$C_x H_{2x} O_x + xO_2 \searrow xCO_2 + xH_2O + \underset{\text{(energy)}}{\text{Heat}}$$

The chlorophyll has the power of extracting energy from the sunlight and storing it in the form of available chemical energy of the carbohydrates. This may be taken as the starting point for the well-known "cycle of carbon" in organic life. By the action of sunlight through the agency of chlorophyll, carbon dioxide is "un-burned," so to speak, and thus serves as a source of free energy either as food or fuel. The free energy of coal and petroleum was extracted from the sunlight which fell upon the vegetation of the earth as it was millions of years ago. Ages later man discovers it and utilizes it for his own purpose of supplying heat and power.

The sunlight which falls upon the grass today gives up a part of its energy to synthesize from water and carbon dioxide those compounds which serve as food for the animal body. In so doing they liberate oxygen to the atmosphere, a process which is reversed when these same compounds are oxidized in living animal tissue and carbon dioxide is given back to the atmosphere as a product of respiration.

Here we see on a large scale in the whole operation of external nature a cycle of balance in chemical reactions that preserves in the environment those fixed conditions which are essential to the maintenance of the dynamic equilibrium of the life process. Moreover, the origin of this cycle goes endlessly back in time through the geological ages of the existence of the earth as a bit of "cosmic dust," during which land and sea and air were being formed to serve as the warp and woof of the fabric in which life weaves the pattern of its infinite variety. The physical energy necessary to drive the pen that forms these words was yesterday stored in the proteins, carbohydrates and fats of food, compounds built up primarily from the air and water and soil by the energy of sunlight and changed by the chemistry of nature into those particular substances that meet the needs of the human body. The day before, so to speak, this same energy was in the white hot mass of the sun as heat, whence, as radiation, it was poured out into space. Its presence in the sun is to be accounted for on whatever theory of cosmic evolution we may accept. The latest theory is that it comes from the release of the subatomic energy of this same carbon atom in the extremely high temperature of the sun. The point is that all the cosmically insignificant events that transpire on this cosmically insignificant planet, including life and the driving of this pen, are linked in an infinite chain of evolution with the present and the past of the vast universe of stars and nebulae. It was no doubt this aspect of reality which was uppermost in the mind of Einstein when he said, "Honestly, I cannot understand what people mean when they talk about the freedom of the human will." As material beings we are part of the material universe, limited in our physical activities by the same sort of physical laws that govern the stars in their courses. We are part of a cosmic machine that science tells us is surely dissipating its available energy toward a final state of complete thermodynamic equilibrium

—a machine which ultimately will be without further supplies of available energy.

Yet as we have tried to suggest, there has apparently been interjected at some point in this universal downhill trend another unknown factor, Life, quite inexplicable in terms of purely physical causation. The evolutionary process in which we find a whole world of mutual adaptations of parts to each other, and of means to apparent ends, seems to run counter to the probabilities of a lifeless world. Ordered groupings of atoms into complex molecules, resulting in the accumulation of free energy and a local and temporary decrease of entropy, run counter to the dissipative processes of decay and combustion. Complex highly-coordinated organisms evolve from less complicated primitive forms. Under the law of increasing entropy, the more probable, less-organized distribution of matter and energy succeeds the less probable. In evolution the reverse is true. Order, in the sense of an arrangement of parts which conform to an apparently purposive pattern, represents the later rather than the earlier point in time. For the individual unit of life, time moves from the materially simple aggregation of the single fertilized cell up through ever increasing stages of organization to the highly-organized coordinated pattern of the adult organism. In the whole scheme of evolution, time's movement expresses itself in the emergence of new forms, seen after the event to have been implicit in earlier forms, though not completely determined by them. In a world of mechanical atoms, the passage from present to future is marked by an increase of the random element. In a living world, time moves from the less to the more highly organized, from randomness to apparently purposeful coordination.

We may illustrate the "entropic" tendency of a lifeless world and the evolutionary tendency in a living world by what would seem to be a fairly accurate analogy. Here is a stream fed from the melting snows far up in the mountains. The difference of level between any two points multiplied by the number of pounds of water per second carried by the current is the power (energy per second) that is potentially available for conversion into useful work. Left to itself the stream dashes over its rocky bed, dissipating its energy in random motion, so that this supply of available energy is not purposefully employed. The net result of the flow is an increase in the total entropy of the universe. Let us suppose that Life is introduced into the situation in the form of the purposeful intent of the human beings who live on the banks of the stream. A dam is built. The water with its available energy is collected in a reservoir, from which it flows in ordered fashion through the turbines of a hydroelectric plant. The available energy in the form of electric current is distributed over the countryside, supplying heat and power to meet the needs of the living beings whose activities interrupted the downhill tendencies of the *non-living* stream. The available energy of the flowing stream ultimately is dissipated as heat, no matter how the power is used. The increase in total entropy is the same as it would have been had the stream been allowed to go its own restless way under the operation of natural laws. *But,* in the building of the dam and in the ordered flow of the water through the turbine, Life arrests the downhill tendency and diverts to its own ends the available energy that would otherwise have been dissipated.

We may carry the analogy a bit farther. Once the supply of available energy has been captured it may be used to attain a wide diversity of vital ends. By *vital* ends is meant ends that make for the adaptation of some organism to its environment. In this particular instance the organism is that most adaptable of all animals, the human species. The power of the stream may be used in the weaving of fabrics, man's substitute for the fur and feathers that life supplies to the beasts and the birds. Or it may be used in carrying out the physical and chemical changes necessary to transform the raw materials of nature into foods for the human body, or into lumber, cement and mortar for its shelter. Life expressing itself as human purpose may direct the flow of energy into a thousand-and-one channels in which it is employed to meet vital needs.

In the analogy we have put into human terms exactly the sort of thing that goes on throughout all of animate nature. In the synthesis of chlorophyll, Life does just what the engineer does when he builds a dam and installs a hydroelectric plant, namely, creates a device for arresting the downhill tendency and a means of storing a supply of available energy. The radiation from the sun is its source. From that storehouse Life draws the energy that it supplies as chemical energy to living things, the grass and the grain and all vegetation. There again it is stored, only to be handed on in turn as food for animals. There it is converted into heat and mechanical movements energizing all of the endless activities of moving creatures, only at long last, through the processes of decay and combustion, to be dissipated as heat in a form no longer available for life's purpose.

Life appears then in the universe, conceived of as a mechanism, as something that defies description in purely physico-chemical terms. Taken as a whole the life cycle does not contravene the law of increasing entropy. In this sense its processes may be described as physical and chemical. But if we undertake to describe in the language of physics and chemistry just *what* it is that determines the successive stages in the whole evolutionary process or to account for the intricate network of nicely balanced reactions between a living organism and its environment, or between the special organs within an organism, we find ourselves lost in a maze of explanations, each of which requires more explanation than does the thing itself. In the organic world each element must be described in terms of its functional relations to other elements. Unity is the key to understanding. The fact that at a certain stage in the downhill process of the cooling earth a highly improbable combination of hydrogen, oxygen, nitrogen and carbon atoms, possessing the unusual properties of protoplasm, should occur, is quite inexplicable if we assume that the Newtonian concepts give a complete description of material being. The advent of two such substances as chlorophyll and haemoglobin, with their unique chemical and physical properties, must be regarded as a miracle from the purely physico-chemical point of view. It is quite inconceivable that they and with them the ordered relationships found throughout the living world should be the result of blind chance operating in an essentially lifeless concourse of atoms and molecules. Life becomes explicable only in terms of purpose, that is, the coordinated activities of related elements to the accomplishment of a specific end—that end being the maintenance and evolution of life itself.

It may be objected that to invoke purpose in explanation of the events of the organic world is scientifically to beg the entire question by introducing into an external situation an element which so far as we know has no existence in nature save in human consciousness. In answer to the objection, it has only to be said that the *understanding* of any phenomenon is essentially the relating of that phenomenon to some fact or group of facts of immediate experience. If we examine critically the fundamental laws of mechanics we will find that exactly this psychological process takes place. For example, Newton's statement that the acceleration in a given direction of a moving body is proportional to the *force* is without meaning to us unless we define the term "force." Our notion of force goes back to the muscular sensation experienced when we exert a push or pull. In getting over the idea of *inertia,* the teacher asks the pupil to imagine the experience of starting or stopping a massive body. There is a certain sort of personification in our speaking of the "pull" of gravity or the "pull" of a magnet for iron. It is just as scientific to personify life and ascribe purpose to its activities as it is to refer the phenomena of electricity and magnetism to the existence of electric and magnetic forces. In both cases we simply interpret one set of happenings in terms of a more immediately experienced set of happenings. In one case we explain the otherwise mysterious movements of bodies by postulating electric or magnetic forces which we understand only by reference to our own muscular sensations. In the other case we account for the observed correlation of events in organic nature in terms of our inner experience of purposive behavior.

We tried to show in Chapter 3 how physical science created an "image world" of inert matter and blind force by abstracting from the immediate stuff of experience those relationships that can be expressed in mathematical language. The entire content of this image world reduces itself to material particles, molecules and atoms, whose properties are defined in terms of the effects which they produce upon each other. Happenings in this world are reduced to transfers of energy between these material particles. These transfers of energy take place in such a way as to decrease the chances that further transfers will occur, that is, in the direction of an increasing randomness in the distribution of matter and energy in the material universe. This image world of physical science corresponds to man's real world in the sense that predictions based on the relationships in the image world are verified with a reasonable degree of precision in the experienced world, thus giving man an increasing control over his material environment.

Physical biology, starting from the physico-chemical concepts of matter and asking its questions in the language of physical and chemical experiments, finds in the organic world nothing but an amazingly intricate network of physico-chemical reactions. Nowhere does the biologist find in living processes any exception to the laws of physics and inorganic chemistry. Matter and energy are conserved, available energy is dissipated, just as in inorganic nature. But everywhere in these processes, he finds a unity in spatial patterns and in time sequences of energy transfers that are entirely beyond prediction in terms of physical causation. He may, for purposes of scientific investigation, isolate an organ or an organism and find all that transpires within explicable in physical and chemical terms; but when he has to account for the means by which these occurrences are maintained as a continuous process, he has to include with the organ or the organism the environmental factors that condition those internal processes. The changes that occur are seen to be within the limits set by antecedent physical causes, but at the same time to be directed to future ends. It is in this latter aspect that life transcends the limits of the "universe of discourse" prescribed by the physics and chemistry of so-called inert matter. In conscious experience this anticipation of future ends in present activity we call *purpose*. In exactly this sense, it seems to me, a scientific understanding of vital processes calls for the assumption of a property in living matter that is not included in the Newtonian concept —namely, a certain inherent inner quality which we may describe by the term "psychical," by virtue of which its behavior is conditioned by the anticipation of future ends as well as by antecedent physical causes. It is only by some such postulate that we can account for the presence of the evolutionary urge in an otherwise mechanically determined world and rationalize what we can only describe as the purposive relatedness that unites all life in a coordinated whole.

Life is often pictured as engaged in an endless struggle with the blind forces of an unfriendly material environment. The "struggle for existence" suggests life as something opposed to the natural order of material being, something injected from without that maintains itself only by ceaseless warfare against unfriendly forces. This conception arises in part from the quality of "inertness" imposed on matter by physical science. By limiting its universe of discourse to those aspects of reality which the intellect can deal with in mathematical terms, atomistic mechanism excludes the possibility of any event, material pattern, or energy transfer that is not completely determined by the past. Therefore life in its creative aspect must appear as something foreign and opposed to the natural order of the physical world, something which must struggle to exist.

When we admit the possibility of the purposive behavior of living matter, the role of life in the material world ceases to be one of opposition to the natural trend. One sees in the downhill tendency of a mechanically running-down world the necessary condition for the expression in objective reality of the inner psychical quality that we have ascribed to matter in living beings. We recognize this at once when we consider the situation at the level of human consciousness. Unless we take the extreme mechanistic view and see human behavior only as the necessary mechanical response of an organism to external stimuli and freedom as pure delusion, we recognize a psychical urge that motivates our present activities for future ends. But this inner urge can only find objective expression through the medium of the energy that is continually supplied to our bodies from the external world in the food we eat and the air we breathe. As we have seen, this energy comes to us as radiation from the cooling sun, a downhill tendency without which all externalized expression of any psychical urge on this planet would be impossible. Looking at it in this way, we see life not as opposed to the natural trend of an ever increasing randomness in the physical aspect of the world but rather as a direct beneficiary of that process. Not only does all life appear as one, but the unity extends itself to include the cosmic fact of the cooling of a star.

So all through organic nature we find living processes maintained by the operation of the universal law of increasing entropy. Thus we see organic evolution and the operation of the second law as not opposing movements in the world. We may think of the evolutionary drive as residing in the psychical property of living matter. As Schopenhauer has expressed it, it is the "World as Will." Its expression in material forms and movements in the dynamic patterns of living beings can only occur through interaction of one portion of matter upon other portions of matter, that is, by the transfer of energy. This transfer of energy can in the long run occur only in such a way that entropy is increased. Therefore, if life is to externalize itself in spatial arrangements of matter and in the dynamic coordination of physical and chemical reactions, it must utilize the entropic tendency of energy. In other words, the psychical aspect of matter can only express itself in mechanistic terms, and therefore mechanism is all that objective science can discover in vital processes.

Perhaps this whole idea of the correlation of the mechanical and the vital, the physical and the psychical, in the world of human experience can best be illustrated by a comparison of the human brain with one of the latest achievements of engineering science, the electrical calculating machine. This is a complicated combination of mechanical counters, controlled and energized by electronic vacuum tubes, that automatically makes in a matter of hours involved numerical computations that would require weeks and even months of time for a trained computer. In a recent paper before a meeting of the American Institute of Electrical Engineers, Professor Warren McCulloch, a neurophysiologist, gave a description in electrical terms of the processes that occur in the ten billion neurons (nerve cells) of the human brain. These processes he finds to be in their physical aspects essentially the same as those taking place in the computing machine. Each nerve cell is like an electronic relay, with its own power supply furnished by the "burning" of the sugar from the blood stream. The interior surface of each cell is thus maintained at a different electrical potential from the outer. Fibers from each cell are intimately interlaced with the fibers of other cells, and electrical impulses are thus transmitted in a step-by-step process from cell to cell, in a manner essentially similar to that in the electrical calculating machine.

There are notable differences, however. The number of neurons in the brain is approximately ten billion. A computing machine with only one thousandth of this number of vacuum tube relays "would require the power of Niagara Falls to operate it and the Niagara River to keep it cool." As elsewhere, the engineers are a long way behind Mother Nature.

A more important difference lies in the fact that there is, in the transmission of electrical impulses from cell to cell in the brain, the possibility of a *selective* action that is not to be found in its electro-mechanical counterpart. In the latter the particular train of action which the electrical impulses follow is determined by the human mind that perforates the cards fed into the machine to control the sequence and character of the individual operations of its electrical and mechanical parts. The machine does what the mathematician *wills* it to do. Without that injection of human purpose it is nothing more than an intricate assembly of electrical and mechanical elements whose movements are as devoid of meaning as are those of waves breaking on a rocky shore. In the brain, on the other hand, there resides not only the mechanism for transmitting the electrical impulses from neuron to neuron, but also the power of selecting and controlling the particular path within the intricate network of billions of neurons by which the stimulus from a sense organ effects some overt response in bodily movement. The living brain has what is from the electro-mechanical point of view the miraculous ability to determine the sequence and character of the physical events that accompany psychical processes. To shift to a more familiar comparison, we may say that the brain serves both as the telephone switchboard and the central operator in the communication system that connects sensory stimuli with motor responses in the human organism.

A still further difference between the brain and a purely physical mechanism is its ability to establish more or less permanent patterns of response among the neurons. In other words, the brain has the faculty of *organizing* the process of transmission of electrical impulses along definite paths. Looked at simply as an electrical network there would be an infinite number of paths that an electrical impulse might take. Thus any stimulus might set up a "chain reaction" that would spread throughout the whole system of neurons, producing, one might suppose, a violent "brain storm." But physiologists tell us that the electrical impulses from one set of neurons may *excite* impulses in a second set and at the same time *inhibit* response in a third set. Due to this fact the brain can exert a selective influence that determines the path which an electrical impulse will take in the maze of nerve cells and fibers. In other words there is introduced into the functioning of the brain an element either of chance or choice. Such an element is impossible if we regard cerebral processes as governed wholly by electrical and chemical factors. There is the further fact that, once a given path is set up, this path is the one most likely to be followed with any recurrence of the original stimulus, and become more firmly established with each repetition. These facts suggest the rough comparison with the formation of paths made through underbrush by a grazing herd. They give us a picture of what goes on throughout the whole nervous system in the formation of mental and behavior habits, the establishment of conditioned responses, and the acquirement of skills.

Now all this points to an inherent capacity within the brain for self-organization, the creation in time of something that, prior to the event, was nonexistent. Whatever explanation in purely physical terms may be given, the fact remains that in the organization of the brain into definite response patterns we have to invoke an extra-physical something that would be designated either as chance or purpose.

The first just doesn't make sense. To ascribe to *chance* the creation of the amazingly intricate complex of neural patterns which must be established in the brain and nervous system of a Horowitz before he can translate the visual sensations produced by the musical score into the series of muscular responses needed for the artistic performance of a piano concerto is as absurd as to say that the thousands of electrical connections in a telephone switchboard just *happened.*

Going still further in this example, there is no conceivable electro-mechanical picture of what went on in the brain-cells of the composer while the musical ideas of his creative purpose were being translated into the visible symbols of the piano score, which in turn initiated the train of nerve impulses and muscular responses that resulted in the physical expression of those ideas in the artist's performance.

Certainly in the material substance of nerve tissue there resides the possibility of producing physical effects from nonphysical causes. But that material substance is composed of the same chemical elements that enter into it from the food we eat and the air we breathe. Therefore unless we assume some miraculous transformation to occur in matter when food is assimilated and becomes the living tissue of an organism, we are compelled to ascribe to the ultimate stuff of the material world potentialities that are beyond the physical and chemical properties of inert matter. These potentialities we have designated as psychical, as distinguished from physical. They are realized in the functional relationships that characterize the vital processes of all organisms and find their highest expression in the psychophysical activities of the human brain. Viewed objectively these activities are physical. Experienced subjectively they are mental. By ascribing psychical as well as physical properties to the ultimate stuff of the world we effect a conceptual synthesis that resolves the dualism of mind *and* matter into a mind-matter concept of reality that permits us to think of the downhill process of the material universe and the creative process of evolution as two aspects of the expression of a living Purpose in a living world. Without the running down process life and mind are impossible. Only in terms of life and mind does that process have purpose and meaning.

We turn next to a consideration of the evolution in scientific thought that came with the study of electrical and magnetic phenomena and the development of the mathematical laws governing them. This led to a synthesis of the phenomena of light and electromagnetism and to the conception of the electrical nature of material atoms and finally to the identification of matter and energy. This evolution of ideas has completely revolutionized the world view of physical science and has rendered atomistic mechanism as obsolete as the pre-Copernican theory of the stellar universe.

CHAPTER 5

Magnetism, Electricity and Light—
a Scientific Trinity

"And God said, 'Let there be light'."

GENESIS I, 3

IN THE PRECEDING CHAPTER we have tried to get a stereosopic view of the two processes which together form the full expression of the external world. Looked at separately, the down hill process summarized in the second law of thermodynamics and the creative process of biological evolution together with the purposeful coordination of function in the individual organism appear as being mutually opposed to each other. Seen together, however, they appear as mutually complementary. Metaphorically we may speak of a life "force" but in so doing we put the distinctive characteristic of the living as opposed to the lifeless in a category that is wholly mechanical and our world view thus becomes completely mechanistic. To avoid this we may, if we choose, speak of a "life intelligence". In order for such a characterization to have any meaning, we have to revise our concept of the final stuff of the world to include both physical and mental properties and, following a perfectly orthodox scientific procedure, we speak of matter as being "psycho-physical".

What we have called "life intelligence" in the lower orders of organisms appears as an automatic adaptation of the living creature to its natural environment. Higher up in the scale, we find intelligent behavior that approximates the same sort of behavior in the human creature. In his fascinating book on "The Mentality of Apes", Köhler describes the intelligence of his simian subjects thus: "What seems to us *intelligence* tends to be called into play when circumstances block a course which seems obvious to us, leaving open a roundabout path which the human being or animal takes as meeting the situation."[1] We seem not to be stretching the meaning of words beyond the elastic limit when we speak of intelligence as being a characteristic property of life processes in general and of matter as possessing psychical as well as physical properties.

In order not to seem to be going off the deep end into scientific mysticism, we turn a moment to a purely physical analogy to illustrate what we mean by the psychical nature of matter. We refer to the polarity exhibited by a magnetized body. Here is an iron rod that in its initial state shows no magnetic properties. It is brought into the field of a powerful magnet or placed inside a coil of wire carrying a direct current of electricity. Immediately the rod becomes magnetized, as shown by its ability to attract or repel other magnets and to hold bits of iron filings at its two ends. Externally the rod is no different in its magnetized condition from what it was initially. Our physics text-books tell us that what happens in the magnetizing process is nothing more than a rearrangement, under the influence of the magnetic field, of the tiny magnetic elements of which the gross body of the rod is composed. Each of these small elements, we are told, is itself a bit of polarized matter and the magnetizing field simply orients each element in the direction of the field so that free magnetisms of opposite signs appear at the two ends of the rod.

In this analogy it is not intended to suggest that the organizing power in the living organism is magnetic. All that is intended is simply this, that in seeking an explanation of the physical fact of the effect of a magnetic field on an iron rod we have to predicate that the stuff of the rod has itself magnetic properties. In like fashion we must assume in accounting for the purposive correlation of function in the

[1] *The Mentality of Apes*, Harcourt Brace, New York, 1925.

living organism that there is a property in the material stuff of the organism that makes it responsive to non-material influence and that property we have called psychical.

Something of this idea is carried over to the whole process of biological evolution and is beautifully stated by Professor J. Arthur Thomson in his Terry Lecture at Yale University in 1924. Speaking of the problem of the origin of life he said: "We must confess that the general trend of evidence is strongly in favor of the belief in a continuity of process from nebula to earth and from cooling earth to awakening life, always supposing however that *mind* is the warp to matter's woof, for in the beginning was Mind, and that Mind is the light of men."[2]

Leaving for the time being the synthesis of the mental and the physical in our biological concepts, we turn to the consideration of the far reaching fusion of ideas that marked the intellectual rise in the fields of magnetism, electricity and physical optics during the nineteenth century. Out of this came the still greater synthesis of the concepts of time and space that was effected in the theory of Relativity in the early years of the present century.

The story of the revolution in scientific thought that came with the amazing growth of experimental knowledge in nineteenth century physics is one of the most thrilling chapters in the history of ideas. We are not thinking so much of the vast changes brought about in the external conditions of the life of civilized man as a result of this growth in scientific knowledge, as of the complete revision of our notions of the nature of the external world that developments in this field have necessitated. Moreover these developments have affected in no small degree our realization of the intimate relation that exists between the physical and the mental. Electricity at rest on an electrically charged body appears as a sort of "dematerialized" matter. The electric charge on a conductor distributes itself strictly according to

[2] *Concerning Evolution,* Yale University Press, 1925.

the mathematical law that would govern the behavior of an incompressible weightless fluid under the action of a Newtonian force. The mathematical beauty and symmetry of the equations of the electromagnetic field generated by electricity flowing through a conductor not only satisfy the demands of the intellect but suggest a correlation between mind stuff and the stuff of matter that spiritualizes the final reality back of sense experience. Here the term "spiritualize" is not used in any religious sense, but simply in contrast to the older scientific procedure of externalizing in a world of inert matter the sources of all sense stimuli.

In this new background the mind finds itself reflected and proceeds to the creation of a mathematical world image far more readily than against a background of hard immutable atoms and mechanical forces. The creation of this world image began with the researches of the Englishman, Gilbert of Colchester, in the latter half of the sixteenth century. The properties of the magnetic needle and their use in the mariner's compass were known to the Chinese as early as the eleventh century. Gilbert studied also the ability of resinous materials when excited by friction to attract and/or repel light objects. To explain the behavior of the compass needle he conceived of the earth as a great magnet with its magnetic pole located in the general region of the geographic north pole. He coined the word *electricity* for the cause of phenomena shown by resinous bodies. Influenced by the scholastic spirit of his time, Gilbert ascribed electric and magnetic forces to the presence of something like a soul which, emanating as an ethereal substance from the electrified or magnetized body, draws neighboring bodies to it. One may note in passing that personification of the causes of the mysterious in Nature was the first step toward understanding by early science just as it is in the primitive mind of the savage.

It was almost a whole century before the next step was taken on the road of discovery. In the interval considerable progress had been made in means for producing heavy charges of what is now called "static electricity". In 1752, Benjamin Franklin's famous experiment of the kite in the thunderstorm had identified the lightning's flash and the thunder's roll with the spark and snap of the discharge of a Leyden jar. (Some over-critical historians raise a question as to whether Franklin himself ever actually performed the experiment. As a matter of fact, his description of its performance in a letter to an English friend is written in the historical present, and does not contain the first person singular pronoun. He does not say in so many words that he *himself performed* the experiment.)

In 1786, Galvani, an Italian physician, made some observations which led to the identification of the electric charge with that other manifestation of electricity, the electric current. In studying the muscular response in a dissected specimen of a frog's legs to mechanical stimulation of the spinal cord, he noticed a spasmodic contraction of the muscles of the leg that occurred with the passage of the spark from an electric machine placed at some distance away on the laboratory table. In his investigation of the phenomenon, he discovered the important fact that if contacts of two dissimilar metals were made at the same time at two different parts of the specimen the same effect was produced as that by the passage of the electric spark. Galvani explained the phenomenon in terms of "animal electricity".

As so often happens, Galvani's facts were all right, but his explanation was wrong. The true explanation was given fourteen years later by another Italian, a physicist this time, Alessandro Volta. He showed that the electric impulse produced by the contacts of the two different metals with the conducting tissue of the frog's body could be duplicated by immersing two plates of different metals, copper and zinc for example, in salt or lye solution. This arrangement is what the high school student of physics today recognizes as the simplest form of the familiar electrical cell, in which chemical energy serves to maintain the energy of a continuous electrical current.

In the same year that Volta's account of his many-celled chemical battery was published in London, two Englishmen, William Nicholson and Sir Anthony Carlisle, used it as a source of electric current and effected the electrolysis of water into its elements, hydrogen and oxygen. It is worth noting that this example of team play between scientific men of different nations is characteristic of the whole spirit of science throughout the Western world up until these recent years when the secret of the destructive power of the atom seems too dangerous to be disclosed even to allies, who may turn to foes. The truly scientific spirit is international in its scope. Two Italians and two Englishmen may well be said to have made the initial discoveries that opened the way for the development of the vast field of electro-chemistry.

We shall, in a later chapter, follow the growth of ideas in this field that ultimately led to the concept of the electrical nature of matter and paved the way for the advance into the field of subatomic physics. Just now we are interested in following that other development that came from the discovery of a chemical means of producing electric energy in the form of an electric current.

Things moved a bit more slowly along the line of electromagnetism than along the line of discovery in electrochemistry. It was not until twenty years after Volta's disclosure of his chemical battery that any headway was made on the puzzling problem of the relation between electricity and magnetism. By this time, orthodox physicists had abandoned the notion of a non-physical explanation of the "action at a distance" shown in both magnetic and electrical attraction and repulsion and were thinking of both magnetism and electricity as "imponderable fluids". While the idea of an imponderable fluid does not go much further for the modern scientific mind than does that of a hypothetical soul in the explanation of the observed physical facts, yet it was quite acceptable in the early years of the nineteenth century. Although the idea of a weightless fluid, phlogiston, advanced by early eighteenth century chemists in explanation of combustion, had blown up in the face of Lavoisier's quantitative experiments, yet the conception was still serving a useful purpose in the current theories of the nature of heat and the processes of heat transfers between hot and cold bodies. But the idea was not particularly useful in accounting for the similarities and also the differences between electrical and magnetic phenomena. The notion of imponderable fluids among physicists of a century and a half ago was something like that of "allergies" among the medical profession of today—a sort of verbal string for tying together a number of unexplained facts.

But as it turned out, the facts did not make a very neat bundle. There were a lot of loose ends that the eager minds of nineteenth century physicists kept pulling at in an unending series of experiments in this fascinating field. The first of these was Hans Christian Oersted, a Dane, who in 1820 performed a series of experiments that tied up two of these loose ends, and established the fact that it is the electric current rather than the electric charge that exhibits magnetic properties. In the light of present knowledge his experiment was simplicity itself. He discovered the fact that a conductor carrying an electric current placed parallel to and above or below a compass needle will cause the needle to be deflected from the magnetic meridian. His experiments showed that the magnetic force is in a plane perpendicular to the direction of the flow of current in the conductor and exerts a force on a magnetic pole that is tangent to the circle that centers in the conductor. He summed up the observed facts as follows:

> "Electric conflict can only act upon
> magnetic particles of matter.

> Electric conflict is not enclosed in the conductor, but is at the same time dispersed into the surrounding space."[3]

Oersted seems to avoid committing himself as to the nature of the interaction between the conductor carrying the current and the magnetic body in his use of the term "conflict". He states that the "magnetic bodies or rather their magnetic particles seem to resist the passage of this conflict and can hence be moved by the impulse of contending forces". He is equally noncommittal as to the nature of electricity itself and refers to it as "electric force or matter" running through the conductor.

Following the publication of Oersted's discovery in 1820, advance in experimental knowledge of electromagnetic phenomena moved forward rapidly. Important contributions were made in both France and Germany during the next ten years. Of these, the most significant for our immediate purpose is the beautiful series of experiments carried out by the French physicist, André Marie Ampère, which showed the mutual attraction of parallel conductors carrying currents in the same direction, their repulsion when the currents flowed in opposite directions. He further showed that the magnetic action of a solenoid, a coil of wire carrying an electric current, is the same as a series of magnetic elements distributed along the straight or curved magnetic line which is encircled by the turns of the solenoid. He showed that a closed electric circuit had the same magnetic properties as a thin shell bounded by the circuit with positive and negative magnetism in equal amounts distributed over the two faces of the shell.

Ampère conceived of a magnet as composed of small elemental magnets, each with its axis parallel to the polar axis of the magnet. Each of these elemental magnets contained equal quantities of the north and south magnetic flu-

[3] *Source Book of Physics,* McGraw-Hill, N. Y., 1935.

ids. Moreover, each of these magnetic "molecules" was in its magnetic behavior the equivalent of a circular electric current, the plane of the circle being at right angles to the axis of the magnetic "molecule." In this way the mutual action between magnets and conductors carrying electric currents was explained in terms of two hypothetical imponderable fluids. Such was the fashion of the scientific thought of the time. It is worth noting that, to Ampère's mind, the mechanics of the situation presented no especial difficulty. How one imponderable fluid flowing in a conductor could exert a mechanical force upon a needle composed of molecules each of which possessed equal quantities of the opposite kinds of a second imponderable fluid was not of any particular importance. The fact that the observed phenomena could be formulated in certain neat mathematical relations was in itself sufficient.

It is interesting, however, to note the change in conceptual background brought about by three centuries of mechanistic interpretation of physical phenomena. Gilbert of Colchester found a satisfactory explanation of magnetic forces acting through space by invoking the idea of an immaterial soul in the magnet. In Ampère's time the idea of soul as an effective cause of material movements was distinctly out of date. An imponderable fluid, and hence in the Newtonian sense an immaterial fluid, was on the other hand quite scientifically orthodox. We must hasten to add that no assumed properties of these imponderables were invoked in explanation of the observed relations—the imponderable electric and magnetic fluids were not used to explain physically *how* electric and magnetic forces act. They were used as a metaphysical cause for the existences of these forces. In short, the imponderables of early nineteenth-century physics had exactly the same status as Newtonian *matter*. Both serve as a conceptual scaffolding, to which the scientific mind may cling, in the building of the image world of mathematical order which it constructs from the chaos of sense experience.

For Newton matter was that whose motion was altered by gravitational and mechanical forces. For Ampère electricity was a fluid whose presence in material bodies gave rise to movements that could not be accounted for by these gravitational and mechanical forces. Both matter and electricity were scientifically defined in terms of certain observed and deduced mathematical relationships. Upon these a system of units and methods of measurement in terms of these units was built up. In fact two self-consistent sets of units were established. One was based on the force of the electric current on a magnetic pole, the other on the mutual force between two bodies carrying static electrical charges. The unit quantity of electricity as defined in the first, the electromagnetic system, turned out to be 3×10^{10} (30 trillion) times as great as the unit quantity as defined in the second or electrostatic system. The significance of the ratio was later to be pointed out by Maxwell in his electromagnetic theory of light.

One notes that the rapid advance in knowledge of electricity and magnetism came not from investigations into their ultimate nature but rather from the development of methods of measuring their quantitative aspects. To call electricity an imponderable fluid might have a certain conceptual value. It had little effect in promoting knowledge of how electric and magnetic phenomena are related. As in the earlier development of mechanics, scientific knowledge was gained by measurement.

Ampère achieved a complete mastery of all the implications of Oersted's discovery of the magnetic effects of the electric current. He left unsolved the converse problem of the production of electrical effects by magnetic means. It was left to the outstanding genius of Michael Faraday, the self-taught son of an English blacksmith, to make this greatest contribution to the new science of electromagnetism. Faraday was not a mathematician. *Understanding* for him did not come with the establishment of mathematical relationships. With superlative skill as an experimenter he combined the highest type of creative imagination, which visualized a mechanical model of the physical relationships back of phenomena. He pictured the forces of magnetic and electric attraction and repulsion as acting along the "curves of force," and the space in which these forces acted constituted the electric or magnetic field. The physical thing back of these forces was resident in this field quite as much as in the material objects, the charged conductor or the magnetized steel, in which, according to the earlier view, the imponderable fluids were supposed to reside. According to Faraday, the magnetic properties of a magnet are to be ascribed not to something within the magnet, but rather to a state which exists in the region about the magnet. He says: "Upon what this state depends cannot as yet be declared. It may depend upon the ether as a ray of light does, and an association has already been shown between light and magnetism. It may depend upon a state of tension or a state of vibration or perhaps some other state analogous to the electric current to which the magnetic forces are so closely related. Whether it of necessity requires matter for its sustentation will depend upon what is understood by the term matter. If that is to be confined to ponderable or gravitating substances, then matter is not essential to the physical lines of magnetic force;—but if, in the assumption of an ether, we admit it to be a species of matter then the lines of force may be some function of it. Experimentally, mere space is magnetic.—It is I think an ascertained fact that ponderable matter is not essential to the existence of physical lines of magnetic force."

Faraday wrote this in 1851, after almost forty years of uninterrupted research in electricity and magnetism, a field in which his creative genius had wrought order and meaning into what had hitherto been chaos and confusion. Faraday's insight came from an imaged model of how phenomena are physically related, rather than from the reasoned derivation of mathematical relations. And it was by virtue of this mental quality that he was led to the idea of the existence of a physical reality that is independent of ponderable matter. In addition to laying the experimental foundation of three great branches of electrical science, electrochemistry, electromagnetic induction, and electric waves, Faraday made an epochal contribution to the conceptual foundation of modern physics when he introduced the idea of "the field of force."[4]

To Faraday's mind it appeared "very extraordinary, that as everywhere electric current was accompanied by a corresponding intensity of magnetic action at right angles to the current, good conductors of electricity, when placed within the sphere of this action, should not have any current induced through them, or some sensible effect produced equivalent in force to such a current." In a masterly series of investigations, he showed that the one thing lacking in previous attempts to observe such an effect was motion of the conductor relative to the magnetic field, or, what was equivalent, a variation of the intensity of the component of the magnetic field at right angles to the conductor. He showed that a steady current in a coil of wire induced no effect in an adjacent coil except as the current in the first coil was *varied* in such a way as to vary the magnetic lines of force that were cut by the turns of the second coil; that a stationary magnet close to a coil produces no induction of electric current, but when the magnet is moved in such a way that the magnetic flux through the coil is increased or diminished an electromotive force will be generated. All of this the high school student of today learns in his elementary physics, and the illustrations in his textbook show the magnet with its field of force, the conductor cutting these lines of force, and an arrow indicating the direction of the induced electromotive force. The student, repeating the experiments that Faraday performed for the first time a hundred years ago, gets the same feeling for the reality of these nonmaterial intangibles that he has for the material objects that he sees and handles.

[4] *Ibid.*, p. 511.

The whole development in the field of electrodynamics—the electrical generator and motor, the telephone, the wireless telegraph and the radio—all evidence the practical reality of something whose existence is wholly inferential. This mind-created reality had exactly the same status as the mind-created matter with its property of mass and gravitation with which Newtonian mechanics deals. Both serve as the conceptual framework into which the mind fits the facts of experience.

Faraday was the Galileo of nineteenth century electrical science. Just as the mind of Newton synthesized the results of Galileo's experiments into a complete mathematical system of mechanics, so did the mathematical genius of Clerk Maxwell sum up the empirical knowledge of electricity and magnetism of the first half of the nineteenth century into a complete theory of the electromagnetic field; and as Newton's mathematics had carried him beyond the experimentally established facts of Galileo's mechanics to the universal law of gravitation, so Maxwell arrived at the electromagnetic theory of light as a mathematical deduction from the theory of the electromagnetic field. Faraday's creative imagination formed the physical picture of the electromagnetic field that combined all the facts of electric charges, electric currents, and the relations of these to magnetic phenomena into a coherent conceptual whole. He surmised that there must be some intimate relation between light and magnetism. Maxwell translated Faraday's physical imagery into the precise definiteness of the electromagnetic field equations and proved mathematically that the effect of an electric disturbance would be propagated as an electromagnetic wave in free space. The velocity of propagation is numerically equal to the 3×10^{10} centimeters per second, a numerical quantity that is the ratio of the electromagnetic to the electrostatic unit quantity of electricity. This ratio turns out to be very close to the measured velocity of light. In a paper published in 1865 entitled "A Dynamical Theory of the Electro-magnetic Field," Maxwell gives his mathematical treatment based on Faraday's ideas of electric and magnetic lines of force. Speaking of the velocity of propagation of the electromagnetic disturbances as waves in free space, he says: "This velocity is so nearly that of light, that it seems we have strong reason to conclude that light itself (including radiant heat and other radiations if any) is an electromagnetic disturbance in the form of waves propagated through the electromagnetic field according to electromagnetic laws. If so, the agreement between the *elasticity* of *the medium* as calculated from the rapid alternations of luminous vibrations, and as found by the slow process of electrical experiments, shows how perfect and regular the elastic properties of the medium must be when not encumbered with any matter denser than air."[5]

Two points of special interest to our study of the conceptual evolution in electrical theory are to be noted. The first is that Maxwell does not abandon Faraday's physical picture of lines of electric and magnetic force and substitute for them the purely mathematical relations of the field equations. Rather he brings that picture into sharp focus, by seeing Faraday's lines of force as stresses residing in a nonmaterial medium that has at least one property of a material medium, namely that of elasticity. The second point is that this physical property of the nonmaterial medium is invoked in explanation of observed physical facts—that the velocity of light is numerically equal to the velocity of propagation of electromagnetic disturbances. In other words, Maxwell builds his conceptual scaffolding into the structure of his completed theory. This was practically useful in that it resolved the difficult problem of conceiving of an elastic solid "ether" having mechanical properties such as to account both for the transverse vibrations of light and for its enormous velocity, while at the same time not affecting in any discernible way the movement of material bodies through it.

[5] *Ibid.*, p. 537.

Maxwell substituted for the luminiferous ether that had been postulated in explanation of the wave theory of light an ether having a dielectric constant and magnetic permeability such as to account for the observed facts of electromagnetism. This electromagnetic ether would also serve as the medium for the transmission of light conceived of as electromagnetic waves. As a result there came into late nineteenth-century physics the concept of a physical reality having certain numerical physical properties and hence a substance in the philosophical sense of the term, and yet not material in the Newtonian sense.

Thus we see the evolution of a new conceptual background that accompanied the revolutionary industrial, economic and social changes brought about by the practical use of scientific discovery in the fields of electricity and magnetism. From Gilbert's hypothesis of a soul in magnetic bodies to account for their strange power of producing motion in other bodies at a distance, through the notion of imponderable fluids, to the Maxwellian conception of an electromagnetic ether as a medium for the transfer of electric and magnetic forces and for the propagation of light, we trace an evolution of thought away from materiality and the purely mechanical conception of physical causation. A something, nonmaterial, comes to be invoked as a link in the chain of physical causation that is assumed to condition all movements of matter. Here we see an example of that tendency of the mind to find satisfaction, that is, to see explanation, when the unfamiliar is reduced to or correlated with the familiar. Action at a distance is not a fact of immediate experience. Tensions, stresses in material bodies, are something that we are aware of in our own muscular sensations. Waves on water and waves in the air are facts of immediate or almost immediate observation. Therefore when we have reduced the apparent action at a distance of electrical and magnetic forces to the stresses in a medium, and, at the same time, are able to account for the speed of light by numerical properties which we have assigned to that medium, the mind is prepared to accept the objective reality of something, the sole evidence for which lies only in the fact that it meets the mind's own necessity for understanding.

Maxwell's conception of the electromagnetic field is a radical departure from the purely mechanical idea that matter is the sole vehicle of energy. Potential energy is stored in the magnetic field that surrounds a conductor carrying an electric current. It is dissipated in the "inductive kick" that occurs when the circuit is broken. In the eight minutes between the departure of radiation from the sun and its absorption at the earth's surface, its energy is presumably free from all material ties. The interstellar ether becomes the storehouse of all the energy that has ever been radiated from the stars. Here we have introduced into nineteenth-century physics the new concept of a substance which is not material and yet serves both as a reservoir for energy and a medium for the transfer of energy between material bodies. This concept was not clearly defined, since it was impossible in Maxwell's time to relate the ether directly to ponderable matter, but nevertheless it was a concept which proved valuable both as mental scaffolding in formulating the mathematical theory and also in stimulating research.

Twenty-two years after the publication of the theory of the electromagnetic field, Heinrich Hertz gave experimental confirmation to Maxwell's prediction in the discovery that the oscillatory discharge of a condenser "spreads out as a wave into space." He succeeded in producing "rays of electric force" and in carrying out with them the elementary experiments which are commonly performed with light and radiant heat. In less than another decade, Marconi had developed the first successful means of utilizing these same electromagnetic waves in the transmission of messages. Today the *ether,* if we use Maxwell's term, or *space,* if we prefer Einstein's description, is packed full of this immaterial energy which, with the snapping of a switch and the turning of a dial, our radio sets convert into the frenzied oratory of a demagogue, the beauty of a symphony, the heroics of "Superman," or the matchless superiority of some brand of toothpaste or canned soup. This same ether is loaded still further with another set of vibrations which with the more elaborate gadgetry of television brings the banalities of Hollywood and the brutality of the prize ring to our very firesides. Thus for most of us, with the exception of the relatively few gifted minds who find in purely mathematical relations adequate explanation without any physical picture, the nonmaterial ether has come to have the same practical substantiality as does the abstract matter which we say we see and feel. Our naive common sense says that if there are undulations, there must be *something* to undulate, just as we say that when we perceive the property of hardness through the sense of touch there must be *something* that we call matter in which this property of hardness resides.

The concept of the ether further stimulated research in the attempts that were made to demonstrate experimentally its existence, properties, and relation to ponderable matter, particularly the question of the relative motion of the ether and matter. In 1729, Bradley deduced from the aberration of the fixed stars the conclusion that the velocity of light must be about 10,200 times that of the orbital velocity of the earth. At this time Newton's theory of the corpuscular nature of light was generally accepted, so that Bradley's explanation of the apparent annual orbital motion of the stars as due to motion of the earth relative to that of the light from the stars offered no difficulty. But with the acceptance of the wave theory, this explanation is tenable only upon the assumption that the ether that transmits the light is stationary in relation to the earth's movement. Hence there must be a relative motion of about 66,000 miles per hour between the earth and the stationary ether.

It is known that the velocity of sound and the velocity

of the air which carries it are additive, that is, if sound travels 1120 feet per second it will travel 1120 plus 10 feet per second with a breeze of 10 feet per second, and 1120 minus 10 feet per second against the breeze. Assuming an ether that is stationary with reference to the earth, the velocity of light relative to the earth should be less when it is propagated in the same direction as the earth's orbital motion than when it travels in the opposite direction. The famous experiment of Michelson and Morley in 1887 was devised for the purpose of detecting and measuring this relative motion. The results were negative. No relative motion was detected, even though the apparatus used was sufficiently sensitive to have detected motion only a fraction of that which the theory of a stationary ether called for.

Here we find the conception of the ether as a physical substance, so useful in electromagnetic theory, leading to an irreconcilable contradiction. The aberration of the stars calls for an ether that is stationary relative to the earth's motion. The Michelson-Morley experiment leads to the conclusion that if there is an ether it must move with the earth in its path around the sun. This was the dilemma which physical science faced at the end of the nineteenth century. This and the impossibility of giving a rational account of the universal fact of gravitation were the outstanding problems of physics at the opening of the new century.

Both problems yielded to the solvent of Albert Einstein's theory of Relativity. In the brilliant light which his mind has focussed on the whole conceptual background of physical reality, it is easy to see that the difficulty lay not only in the hypothesis of a physical ether but in the fundamental Newtonian concepts of time and space. One says the "Newtonian concept," but as a matter of fact the notions of absolute time and absolute space which are the basis of Newtonian mechanics cannot be properly ascribed to Newton. In the *Principia* he only stated what seemed obvious and universally accepted when he postulated that time is "absolute, true and mathematical—taken in itself and without relation to any material object, it flows uniformly of its own nature—absolute space, on the other hand, independent by its own nature of any relation to external objects, remains always unchangeable and immovable." That was the metaphysical background of scientific thought in Newton's day, first formulated by Aristotle two thousand years before. Material objects exist independently of time and space. Time, space and matter are the three independent absolutes back of phenomena to which physical happenings are to be numerically related. Space was a fixed three-dimensional framework, through which time flowed continuously and uniformly. Absolute motion is the change of a material body's position in absolute space; relative motion is its change of position relative to some other body considered as a fixed position of reference.

It is quite foreign to our purpose to attempt an exposition of the theory of Relativity. What we are concerned to point out is the fact that Relativity completely revolutionized the fundamental concepts of physical science. Absolute space and absolute time were shown to be concepts devoid of physical meaning, since no physical experiment can be devised to prove their independent existence. Our notion of space in the physical sense comes from the use of the measuring rod—a material object. Physical time, the time that is measured by our clocks is a numeric given by the periodic movement of a material body through space. The velocity of a material object must of necessity be a velocity relative to some other object or set of objects. The aberration of the stars reveals not the motion of the earth relative to a stationary ether, but its motion relative to the stars. The velocity of light in space is not the velocity of a material something relative to material bodies, since experiment shows that its velocity is constant independently of the relative velocity of the source and the observer. The velocity of light is a constant of nature, and this constancy is inherent in its electromagnetic nature. Space and time are not two independent absolutes. Together they constitute a four-dimensional continuum (three dimensions of space and one of time) in which the time relation of events is conditioned by their space relation because of the fixed and finite velocity of light. The point in time which we call *now* must be specified in connection with a point in space which we call *here*. The length of a measuring rod is not an absolute thing, since it will depend upon the velocity with which it moves relative to the frame of reference. A perfect clock will appear to run too slow if it is moving away from the observer, too fast if it is moving toward him.

Gravitation is not a pull of attraction between two portions of matter, but rather the result of a "warpage," so to speak, which matter produces in the space-time continuum. The three-dimensional geometry of Euclid, which serves perfectly well for a space divorced from time, fails when applied to the relations of a four-dimensional space-time, just as a Mercator's projection of the spherical surface of the earth is misleading as a guide to extended travel over its surface. Einstein gives up the physical picture of an ether that transmits light waves as the air transmits sound, a necessary procedure if one accepts the logical implications of the Michelson-Morley experiment. In so doing and in his rigorous analysis of the fundamental concepts of physics, Einstein created a new "image world" free from internal contradictions and one in which gravitation appears not as an esoteric force, but rather as a mathematical necessity of the geometry of the space-time continuum.

For Einstein the key to the understanding of the phenomena of nature is the pure mathematical construction by which we establish underlying concepts and discover the laws connecting them, to which the data of experience and their mutual relations are to correspond.

By the "data of experience" Einstein meant, as a physicist always means, the numerical data obtained by physical measurements. Thus the warping of space-time by matter as an explanation of gravitation involved the corollary that light should also be subject to gravitation. Therefore rays of light from the stars should be deflected in passing through the intense gravitational field close to the sun. This deflection, if it occurs, can only be detected at the time of a total eclipse of the sun. Hence the eagerness with which astronomers planned to photograph the star field in the neighborhood of the sun at the moment of the total eclipse in 1919. The fact that the images of the stars whose light passed close to the sun's disc were displaced on the photographic plates with reference to the other stars in the field by just the amount that the Einstein theory predicted was hailed by the scientific world as proof that the theory was true.

Thus from the postulate of a *soul* in explanation of electric and magnetic forces, through the idea of imponderable fluids, and the later concept of stresses in a physical but nonmaterial ether, science has finally arrived at a mathematico-physical concept of inanimate nature, wherein the ultimate reality resides in the mathematical relations expressed in Maxwell's equations and the field equations of the general Relativity theory. The three independent absolutes of space, time and matter have been merged into a single system of mathematical relations, in which each has meaning only in terms of the other. In this has been taken a vast stride in the unification of the basic conceptual elements of physical reality.

Back of the pluralistic world of physical events is a unified world of mathematical relationships in which the intellect finds itself—a rational world in which the tension between self and not-self is released, a world of pure ideas not far removed in its essence from the ideal world of Platonic philosophy. The cycle of human thought, beginning with the Greek metaphysic in which the absolute is postulated as the basis of the contingency of sense experience, paradoxically enough is completed in the theory of Relativity

—a theory in which reality resides in the unconditioned relationships of the free field equations. But the cycle is better represented as a turn of a spiral, for, in the course of departure from and return to the Platonic view, the mind achieved a tremendous physical mastery which pure Platonism never contemplated. But more than this, the mathematico-physical image world of Einstein rests upon a foundation of physical experiment. Contrast Einstein's dictum, "All knowledge about reality begins with experience and terminates in it," with the Platonic notion of the illusory quality of all sense experience. For Plato the world existed in the Divine Mind, and those elements of rational order which we can discern in it arise from the intelligence of that Mind. Therefore the only approach to ultimate reality is by way of the process of rational thought. The complete acceptance of this point of view by the thinkers of the first sixteen centuries of the Christian era led to speculative scholasticism and scientific sterility. Einstein, heir of four centuries of achievements in experimental physical science, started with the assumption of the objective validity of a certain type of sense experience, namely scientific measurement, and proceeded to re-examine the metaphysical background of physical theory. Reconstructing the conceptual framework on this assumption and adopting a geometric construction consistent therewith, he arrived at a unified mathematical theory that finds its justification in the correspondence between its logical implications and observed facts.

The outstanding contribution of Greek thought to a scientific world view was Euclidean geometry. Starting from certain basic propositions called "axioms" and proceeding according to the necessities of logical deduction, Euclid arrived at a self-consistent body of theorems of relationships between mathematical points, lines and figures. This system consists of propositions which follow one from another with such logical rigor that none of them admits of the slightest doubt. The practical justification of geometry rests in the fact that its deductions correspond to the physical relations established by the processes of measurement. In quite parallel fashion Einstein, starting with certain axiomatic (i.e., not rationally deducible) concepts and laws regarding time, space and matter, and proceeding according to the strictly logical processes of a non-Euclidean geometry, arrives at a set of mathematical relations which correspond to the experimentally established facts of the gravitational and the electromagnetic fields in free space, and lead to definite conclusions about the physical universe that are left unexplained in the older theories.*

Einstein reduced the physical facts of gravitation and the electromagnetic field to a matter of the geometry of four-dimensional space-time. In so doing he took an important step toward a complete synthesis between the purely mental processes of mathematical thinking and the relatedness that is the structure of the physical world. Certainly a multi-dimensional geometry is a creature of the mind, and the calculus of imaginaries can not be conceived to be anything but a pure creation of the intellect. And yet we find that with these tools Einstein was able to fashion a theoretical framework in which the facts of gravitation and electromagnetism fit as parts of a mathematical system.

The proposition that this correlation between the mathematical structure of Relativity theory and the observed facts of field physics implies that the order of nature is essentially mathematical cannot of course be proven. But from Copernicus to Einstein the great minds that have broadened the horizon of man's physical universe and increased the depth of human insight into the laws that govern the world of

* The three criteria of the validity of the general theory of Relativity are the shift of the perihelion of Mercury, displacement of the apparent position of the stars at the edge of the sun's disc, and the shift toward the infrared of spectrum lines from a source in a strong gravitational field. In *The Logic of Modern Physics* P. W. Bridgman suggests that the success of the general theory of Relativity is to be ascribed to Einstein's physical insight in the handling of his mathematical treatment rather than to the essentially mathematical structure of nature.

phenomena have been thoroughly imbued with the faith that this is true. Said Kepler, "Nature loves simplicity and units," and in the strength of this faith he devoted years of patient labor to the mathematical study from which he deduced the laws of planetary motion that later were included in the more comprehensive scope of Newton's mechanics.

In Relativity we have an integrated world-view in which mathematical concepts and laws, the rational functioning of the mind, become identified with physical concepts and physical laws. The physical is dissolved in the mental. Neither is lost, but the intimate union of the two gives us a liquid, mobile world of mental relationships in place of the hard, impenetrable, externalized world of material atoms held together by mechanical forces.

Medieval thought accepted the physical cosmos as an expression of Absolute Mind and sought along the paths of metaphysical speculation to find God, the "Unmoved Mover," the source of all being. Its theology sought to effect a synthesis of this metaphysical concept with the Father-God of Jesus' teaching. In the last four centuries of the evolution of physical science, the belief in a divine order predicated on the existence of a Divine Mind has been gradually supplanted by a scientific faith in a rational order of mathematically expressible physical laws. With the accumulation of scientific knowledge and the resultant mastery of physical forces, the metaphysical aspects of reality faded more and more from the world-view of western thought. The pious scientist might retain Deity as an object of religious contemplation. He abandoned the idea of God as being quite unnecessary in physical theory. God as an "Unmoved Mover" would not fit into a world of material atoms in which energy gained by one portion of matter must be at the expense of an equal quantity of energy lost by other matter.

Relativity theory grew out of the scientific necessity of resolving the internal contradictions that resulted from a purely physical picture of reality. It was not imposed on physics by any philosophical demand from without. Physics had to untie a knot of its own making. The result was the substitution of the mathematical model of Relativity for the older mechanical model of atomistic mechanism. In the mathematical model the ultimate realities are mathematical relationships. We thus find ourselves quite reluctantly facing the question of what we mean by the *reality* of these relationships. We have no intention of plunging into the deep waters of what the philosophers call the problem of "being." Death by drowning would be the inevitable fate of one who has never learned to swim in these waters. But it would seem to be a safe statement that the relations of the mathematical model are *mental* realities inherent in the structure of rational mind.

It is perhaps an act of religious faith, but certainly not of irrational faith, to take the next step and to say that the physical realities, symbolized in the mathematical model, are mental realities of exactly the same sort and that these realities exist in the rational mind of the physical universe. Hence the mathematical realities of the field equations and the physical reality of the field itself are one in essence. For individualized mind, these realities can find expression only in symbolic representation. In the universal mind their expression is the physical universe. Pure thought in the mind of man *creates* the mathematical model. Pure thought in the mind of God creates the physical world. One would better say, pure thought in the mind of God *is* the physical universe, since *creation* connotes a temporal sequence from non-being to being, whereas *time* in Relativity theory assumes a spatial rather than a sequential meeting. In the universe as a whole time as conceived in the sequence of physical events has no meaning. This latter concept arises from the partial and interior view which finite individual mind must take of the universe. Universal Mind is subject to no such limitation. The *here* and *now* of finite mind is replaced by *everywhere* and *always* in the mind of God.

We have characterized the inference of a Universal Mind as an act of rational religious faith. I believe that careful analysis will show that, unless we take this step from the physico-mathematical view of Relativity, we are forced to the Berkelian view that denies the objective existence of any substantial reality back of sense experience, and find ourselves driven into the solipsism of David Hume. Either the realities symbolized in the equations of field physics exist in the Universal Mind, or else their existence is limited to the individualized mind in which they are perceived. So far as I can see, the acceptance of either alternative is a matter of choice. From the practical scientific point of view the results are the same, except that the latter places us back in a world in which we must accept the ultimately illusory quality of all sense experiences, including those of scientific measurement.

But the essence of scientific faith is the assurance that the physical world has an objective existence. Its goal is the penetration of the veil which the limitations of our perceptual organs cast over the objects of experience to the ultimate reality behind them. In a measure Relativity achieves that goal in a symbolic construction. Belief in the objective existence of that which is symbolized necessitates at the same time a belief in the existence of a Universal Mind in which symbol and substance are identified. Either that belief, or the acceptance of the whole physical theory as a fabric of human self-deception, would seem to be two alternatives which the physico-mathematical picture offers. As between the two the whole history of physical science proclaims the former as scientifically the more acceptable. Scientific faith insists that nature is *not* one gigantic hoax set up to deceive the questing mind of man. Finding that physical theory, in order to be free from internal inconsistencies, must reduce the external world to a world of mental realities, all scientific tradition indicates that scientific faith will accept the corollary of a Universal Mind in which these realities have their existence.

Scientific faith in the rational order of nature and religious faith in a Divine Mind thus come to have a common object.

I know of no better statement of the position that scientific thought is coming to assume than that given by Professor Hermann Weyl in the Terry Lectures for 1931. "The ultimate foundation for the ratio governing the world, we can find only in God; it is one side of the Divine Being. Thus the ultimate answer lies beyond all knowledge, in God alone; flowing down from him, consciousness, ignorant of its own origin, seizes upon itself in analytic self-penetration suspended between subject and object, between meaning and being. The real world is not a thing founded in itself, that can in a significant manner be established as an independent existence. Recognition of the world as it comes from God cannot, as metaphysics and theology have repeatedly attempted, be achieved by cognitions crystallizing into separate judgments that have an independent meaning and assert definite facts. It can be gained only by symbolic construction."[6]

Here speaks one of the most profound and creative mathematical minds of our day. The unity in the order of pure thought and the unity in the order of the world stem from a common source. Both flow from the one divine Reality which in its unity is both object and subject. Apprehended inwardly this Reality is the "self," the observer who can never be severed from the thing observed. Externalized it is the order of Nature that is recognized in the symbolic construction that is the "image world of science." Thus God, the "thinking self," and the universe of space-time form a trinity, each term of which has meaning only in terms of all.

Here again we must emphasize the difference between "explanation" in the scientific sense and "understanding" in the sense of relating the thing explained to immediate experience. The symbolic construction of the field equations *explains* gravitational and electromagnetic phenomena to the

[6] *The Open World,* Yale University Press, New Haven, 1932, p. 28.

mind of the mathematical physicist. He can *understand* the objective existence of that which is symbolized only through a belief in the existence of a Universal Mind to which what we call physical reality bears the same relation as the symbolic representation bears to his own thinking mind. Thought in the finite mind of man creates the symbolic relations of the mathematical model. Thought in the mind of God constitutes the realities that are symbolized. "Thought" and "mind" for the individual are both matters of immediate experience. The Mind and Thought of the Universe are of the same essence as the mind and thought of the individual. Newton postulated the existence of God "who endures forever and is everywhere" as the metaphysical basis for his assumption of absolute time and space. Relativity leads to the necessity of a Universal Mind as the basis for a belief in the objective reality of that which is symbolized in the mathematical theory.

Chapter 6

The New Physics—Matter and Energy, a Scientific Unity

"The history of science in the twentieth century is one of progressive renunciation of the purely human angle of vision."
Sir James Jeans[1]

"The physicist thus finds himself in a world from which the bottom has dropped clean out; as he penetrates deeper and deeper it eludes him and fades away by the highly unsportsmanlike device of just becoming meaningless."
P. W. Bridgman[2]

In the preceding chapter, we have traced the evolution of scientific thought brought about by the expansion of experimental knowledge of the facts of electricity, magnetism and light. This evolution culminated in the theory of Relativity, in which the contradictions involved in the concepts of a physical ether and physical matter were resolved by substituting for the Newtonian abstractions of absolute time, absolute space and independent matter, the mathematical concept of a space-time continuum in which the existence of matter is symbolized by certain components of curvature of the continuum. This leads to an image world of mental realities. Since "mental realities" have no meaning apart from mind, we are forced to one of two conclusions, either that the ultimate reality of the physical world exists only in the finite mind of the mathematician, or in a Universal Mind co-existing in space-time with the universe itself. The choice of the latter was characterized as an act of "scientific faith"—

[1] *The New Background of Science.* Macmillan, New York, 1934.
[2] "Scepticism, Pragmatism and Truth." Harper's Magazine, March, 1929.

that is, a faith in the external reality of the objects of physical science. Just as the scientific fact of organic evolution, of biological adaptation and the apparent purposiveness of the physico-chemical reactions occurring in vital processes led us to the conception of a psychical quality, a potential "aliveness" in matter, so the synthesis of our knowledge of the electromagnetic and the gravitational fields has brought us to the concept of a cosmic Mind as the matrix of the mathematical relationships of field physics.

We have still the question of the synthesis of the Universal Mind that we have accepted as a necessary postulate for the objective existence of the mathematical realities symbolized in the Relativity theory of time and space and that other abstraction, *matter*, as the substantial background and origin of all sense experience. It is to be stated at once that science has not yet arrived at that complete synthesis. Physical science faces exactly the same inscrutable enigma in the mind-matter relationship of the universe, which confronts each of us as conscious material beings when we contemplate the mystery of the relation of the conscious self to the material body with which it is associated. The universe as mind expresses itself to our finite intellects in the symbolic language of mathematical theory, a changeless, timeless unity. As matter, it impresses itself upon us through the medium of the senses as a world of infinite variety and endless change, a vast concourse of atoms and electrons. Relativity theory gives us as the ultimate reality a space-time continuum, a universal mind, whose changeless content is the mathematical realities symbolized in the field equations. It gives no account of the atomistic aspect of reality, or of the constant transfers of energy going on between material particles, which is generalized in the second law of thermodynamics. Neither does it account for the series of progressive changes in organic nature we characterized as evolution. The only attribute that needs to be ascribed to the Universal Mind in which the mathematical relationships of field physics exist is that of pure intellect—static and timeless in both the evolutionary and the entropic conception of the term. It is the rational contemplative mind of the mathematician, not the restless driving mind of the creator. It is but one aspect of the God in which things "live and move and have their being."

To keep within the universe of discourse of science we must put the problem in the language of physical concepts. So stated the question is: "What is the relation between the space-time continuum that correlates the gravitational and the electromagnetic fields and the microscopic atoms of material bodies?"

Here the age-old metaphysical problem of the one and the many presents itself in physical science as the problem of the existence of individual particles of matter, electricity and energy in a space-time continuum, and it is just for this reason that physicists in the last decade or so have had to become metaphysical and to examine with critical care their fundamental concepts.

It is our purpose to see how the material atom as conceived at the beginning of the present century has gradually dissolved into much the same sort of mathematical relatedness as did the ether in the light of Einstein's analysis. Turning to the elementary textbooks of only a generation ago, we find the atom defined as the smallest particle of an elementary substance that can exist. It was the last step in the process of division of matter. It was pictured, I suspect, as a particle so small that it couldn't be any smaller. It had mass and it occupied space, and since it had no parts it was thought of as occupying its portion of space completely. Unoccupied space between two atoms was possible, but unoccupied space within an atom did not exist.

Electricity on the other hand was conceived of as something infinitely divisible, an incompressible fluid, not atomic in its microscopic structure. The electric charge was defined in terms of the field to which its presence gave rise, the electric current in terms of the magnetic field that surrounds it. However, from the time of Faraday's researches on the passage of the electric current through conducting solutions of certain chemical compounds, it was recognized that the laws of electrolysis could most easily be explained on the assumption that electricity is divided into definite elementary portions which behave like atoms of electricity. Moreover, the fact that the flow of an electric current in a conductor is always accompanied by the generation of heat suggested that there must be some action of the hypothetically imponderable fluid upon the material particles of the conductor. Such an effect can hardly be explained without visualizing *particles* of electricity whose movements in a conductor somehow react mechanically on the atoms of the conductor.

It was only in the latter half of the last century, with the study in that fascinating field, the conduction of electricity through rarefied gases, that the existence of electricity apart from matter began to be suspected. The beautiful effects observed upon the discharge in tubes containing gases at low pressure were matters of passing interest, but were not considered of great scientific importance until the last decade of the nineteenth century. It was observed that as the gas pressure in a glass tube fitted with electrodes was gradually lowered the visible effects were confined to a luminous glow originating at the cathode or negative electrode, and a state of fluorescence on the opposite wall. The nature of these cathode rays was for years a matter of debate. The fact that solid objects placed in their path inside the tube cast a distinct shadow, and the fact that they could be deflected by a magnetic field as a stream of negatively charged particles would be deflected, led to the belief that they were of this character. In 1895 Röntgen of Munich discovered that when these rays generated in a high vacuum fell upon a metal plate, a second type of ray was produced, which he showed had the power to pass through many bodies opaque to ordinary light. Uncertainty as to the nature of these secondary rays, whether they were wave-like as is visible light or were electric particles, led their discoverer to call them X-rays. Subsequent research has shown them to be radiation differing from light only in the matter of their wave length. They constitute one portion of that series of electromagnetic waves that includes at one end the radio waves that may be thousands of yards in length, down through the short radio waves, the microwaves of radar, the infrared, the visible spectrum, the ultraviolet, the Schumann light, then through a whole gamut of X-rays of decreasing wave length and increasing penetrating power to the gamma rays of radioactive substances — and finally, at the extreme short wave length end of the series, the still mysterious cosmic rays.

Röntgen's discovery may well be said to mark the beginning of the New Physics that has completely revolutionized the whole scientific conception of the nature of matter and electricity—a revolution so profound as not only to focus the whole interest of physical scientists upon a new set of problems, but to call for a thoroughgoing reconstruction of the conceptual foundations of physical science itself. The last decade of the last century and the first of the present century comprised a period of intense activity in the new field. In 1897 J. J. Thomson, at the Cavendish Laboratory in England, established the fact that the cathode ray is a stream of particles carrying charges of negative electricity, and that the ratio of electric charge to the mass particle is of the order of two thousand times as great as the ratio of the electric charge carried by the hydrogen ion in electrolysis to the mass of the hydrogen atom. This meant either that the charge of each particle was about two thousand times that of the charge of the hydrogen atom, or else that the mass of the electrical particle was one two-thousandth that of the hydrogen atom which, according to all previous theory, was the smallest possible material mass. Thomson took the latter view, namely that the mass of the individual particle composing the cathode ray was much smaller than the smallest atom and that its charge was the same as the charge on the hydrogen atom in electrolysis. He called these particles "corpuscles."

This was the beginning of the end of the older atomic theory, and the beginning of the theory of the electrical nature of matter, and the conception of the atomic nature of electricity. By the end of the century Thomson's interpretation was found to be the correct one—in the corpuscles of the cathode ray we have particles many fold smaller than the smallest atom, each bearing a fixed and definite electric charge, the atom of negative electricity, later christened the "electron".

It is an interesting fact in the history of science that the revolutionary discoveries that radically alter the trend of scientific thought seem seldom to originate from a single source. They seem to emerge almost simultaneously from different minds working in different fields, as though driven to expression by some common impulse from the depths of the unknown. Perhaps it is enough to say by way of explanation that scientific thought is not the product of a single mind but the joint product of many minds directed toward the same object or set of phenomena, and that it is entirely natural that the same idea should germinate at the same time in the minds of different scientists, just as seedlings in a seed bed thrust themselves at the same time through the earth that covers them. There may be nothing more esoteric than this about it, but certain it is that, during the late nineties and the first decade of the new century, there was a series of discoveries which conspired not only to explain each other but to find a common explanation in the new concept of the electrical nature of matter. Just when physical science had settled itself with a certain measure of complacency in a conceptual world of atomistic mechanism, governed by the great generalizations of the conservation principle and the law of increasing entropy and had found in the laws of the electromagnetic field an apparently adequate explanation of optical phenomena, there appeared upon the scene a group of new actors who called for a new setting of the stage of scientific thought.

We shall not attempt any systematic account of these discoveries any more than to point out in what widely divergent branches of physics they arose. We have already mentioned the discovery of the Röntgen rays and the identification of the cathode rays as negatively charged particles. In 1896 Zeeman in Holland observed the broadening of spectral lines in an intense magnetic field, from which Lorentz was able to calculate a ratio of electron charge to electron mass very nearly the same as Thomson's value. In the same year Becquerel, in France, reported radiations from uranium compounds that passed through material layers opaque to ordinary light and rendered the air conducting, thus hastening the loss of charge of electrified bodies. Four years later, Pierre and Marie Curie succeeded in extracting from pitchblende a salt of a new element nine hundred times more radioactive than uranium. To this new element they gave the name radium. Radioactivity found its explanation in the assumption that almost infinitesimally small numbers of the heavy atoms of the radioactive body are constantly disintegrating, and that the heat and radiant energy continuously generated come from the internal energy of the atoms set free by these atomic explosions. The results of these explosions were found to be of three kinds, A—particles, later shown to be atoms of helium, B—particles identified with electrons and C—rays, which proved to be X-rays of very great penetrating power. Through a series of these changes, the radioactive atom loses a portion of its mass and constituent electrons, and, in the case of uranium, ends up after some fifty billion years as lead. The old notion of the chemical atom as the ultimate constituent of matter likewise had come to its end, and the ancient dream of the alchemists that one element might be transmuted into another was realized in a quite unexpected way.

Having once been recognized for what it is, the electron appeared all over the place. Richardson and others discovered its emission by heated metals, the thermionic effect, which every electrically minded schoolboy today knows about in the electron vacuum tubes of his radio set. Metal plates illuminated by ultraviolet or by visible light emit electrons, as in the photoelectric cell. The wired and wireless transmission of photographs, television and a score of practical uses make this discovery of forty years ago a commonplace today.

While the size of the electron is far below the limits of vision with even the most powerful microscope, yet when projected with sufficient energy through air saturated with water vapor it leaves a trail of fog. These trails, as they are affected by electric and magnetic fields, tell many of the characteristics of the particles. There thus is a sense in which electrons, protons and other subatomic particles that have been discovered since the electron are more nearly directly observed than are molecules or atoms. It is less an act of faith to believe in the actual existence of the electron after having seen a fog trail in a Wilson expansion chamber than to believe in the chemical atom. If we can't see electrons, we can certainly see where they have been.

The period 1900 to 1914 covered the birth and growth to surprising maturity of the electrical theory of matter. In 1912 Laue suggested that if X-rays are light of extremely short wave length, then the presumably geometrical arrangement of the atoms of crystals should produce the same diffraction effects as the regularly spaced parallel scratches of a diffraction grating produce upon light waves. Experiments showed this to be the case and supplied a means of measuring not only the wave lengths of X-rays, which proved to be the order of 1/10,000 of the wave length of visible light, but also made it possible to meaure the atomic spacings of the atoms as well as the actual dimensions of the atoms themselves. Physics thus entered a new field, the field inside the atom, a field infinitesimally small in comparison with any object revealed by the most powerful microscope, but very large in comparison with the size of the electron. Rutherford, in 1911, first proposed the idea of the nuclear or planetary atom. This pictures the atom as something in the nature of a planetary system, with a central nucleus bearing a positive charge and with one or more electrons in orbital motion about it. The nuclear charge is equal to the sum of the electron charges. The simplest atom, hydrogen, consists of a nucleus, the proton, having a unit positive charge and one planetary electron. Since the mass of the electron is only about 1/1800 of the mass of the hydrogen atom, it follows that the mass of the atom is practically that of the nucleus. The radius of the nucleus, however, is about 1/100,000 of the radius of the whole atom, so that the atom, hitherto conceived of as solid, consists largely of empty space. Someone has calculated that the portion of the hydrogen atom that is occupied by the nucleus is about the same proportion of the total volume of the atom as a pencil point is of the total volume of a large lecture hall. This transforms the atom from an impenetrable bit of solid matter to a central nucleus in which most of the atomic mass is concentrated, surrounded by its outriders of electrons. The chemical properties of the atoms of the different chemical elements depend upon the electron outriders, their number and the stability of the electrical system that together with the nucleus they comprise. Their number in turn is determined by the total positive charge carried by the nucleus.

In the earlier years a degree of correlation was found between the nuclear charge and the atomic weight. The reason for the relation between atomic weights and chemical properties of the elements, first pointed out by Mendeleeff and Meyer in the Periodic Table a half century earlier, began to appear. But more important still, since electric charge comes always in unit packages, it follows as a likely hypothesis that the nuclei of all the chemical elements are built up of integral numbers of a common unit, possibly the nucleus of hydrogen, the lightest of the elements. This idea was first advanced by Proust in 1815. Although many of the elements have atomic weights very nearly integral multiples of the atomic weight of hydrogen, yet there are a considerable number which depart widely from the rule. These exceptions made Proust's hypothesis untenable in view of the older conception of the atom. In 1910 Soddy suggested that supposedly elementary substances, whose atomic weights are not approximately integral, are really mixtures of elements of slightly different atomic weight having the same, or nearly the same, chemical and physical properties.

To the chemists, this idea was revolutionary and almost absurd, for atomic weight determinations had been the subject of the most careful and skillful work in the whole field of quantitative chemistry, and it was unthinkable in the chemical tradition that two elements might have different atomic weights and yet be so closely alike in their properties as never to have been separated. Even less likely was it that these two elements should always be present together in proportion so nearly constant as always to give the same apparent atomic weight to the mixture. But the New Physics, in the action of electric and magnetic fields on the charged subatomic particles, had a far more precise method of determining their relative weights than the finest chemical balance. It has been shown that Soddy's surmise was correct, that non-integral atomic weights result from mixtures of components called isotopes. The weights of these isotopes are in all cases very close to exact integers, and the now known chemical elements and their isotopes practically fill the series of natural numbers from 1 to 242. The world of matter with its infinite variety of physical and chemical properties has been reduced to combinations of elemental particles of a few species.

In addition to the proton and electron of the earlier

years of electron theory, the physicists have discovered other components of the atomic nucleus besides the proton—the *neutron*, which has the same mass as the proton but no electric charge, the *positron*, the positively charged counterpart of the electron, and the *neutrino*, a somewhat hypothetical particle with mass of the same order of magnitude as that of the electron but with zero electrical charge.* With their so-called "atom smashing" devices, the cyclotron and the electrostatic generator, physicists are now able to bombard material targets with subatomic particles having velocities corresponding to millions of electron-volts, thus destroying the stability of the atoms of the target, and rendering them radioactive. This induced radioactivity is similar to the natural radioactivity of radium, and its end result is one or more chemical elements, or isotopes, that are different from the element that was bombarded. Thus the neutron bombardment of a target of aluminum will render it artificially radioactive. The nuclei of some of its atoms become unstable and disintegrate. One product of this disintegration is an isotope of sodium known as "radio-sodium". This latter has all the chemical properties of the natural sodium that is a constituent of common salt, but it possesses radioactive properties that persist for a matter of some fifteen hours after its creation. (The term "creation" is used advisedly, since nowhere in the world does radio-sodium exist as a natural substance.) Since radio-sodium has the same chemical properties as ordinary sodium, and since compounds of the latter are present in the human body, it has proved to be an invaluable aid in the study of the body chemistry. All told, some five hundred unstable nuclear species have

* As of March 1952, the latest returns from the subatomic front puts the total number of particles that go to make up the nucleus of the atom at twenty-one. At least that is the number so far identified in the debris from atomic explosions shown by tracks in various Wilson cloud chambers. Since the discovery of the neutron in 1932, the physicists' picture of the inside of the atomic nucleus has grown increasingly more complicated and hope of the discovery of what holds it together has become more and more remote.

been observed, and their value in medicine and other fields of research can hardly be overestimated.

For the physicist and chemist of forty years ago, the transmuting of aluminum into sodium was an undreamed-of possibility. The transmutation of the chemical elements is a commonplace in present-day physics.

We have followed only one line of the development of scientific thought that began with the discovery of the X-ray, the electron and radioactivity at the beginning of the century—the absorbing quest of the internal structure of the atoms. The rapidity with which new phenomena have appeared and have been fitted one after the other into a consistent whole is without parallel in the whole history of human thought. Not a decade nor even a year is an appropriate unit of time in recording this development, but rather a month—and this has come not as the work of one master mind, but of many minds widely scattered over the civilized world. Science in the free world has achieved a unity of ideals and purpose, with resulting achievement that makes idea of a "group mind" seem altogether plausible.

The New Physics has been concerned not only with the problem of the atom. Granted that material atoms are made up of dynamically stable configurations of protons, neutrons and electrons, just what are protons, neutrons and electrons made of? Has not science simply pushed the question back a step from atoms to electrons and protons? Is the question of the relation between matter and electricity any nearer solution because of our discovery that they are both corpuscular in character and always come done up in standard-sized packages, and that there are a relatively small number of different kinds of packages?

The scientist's answer to this question is in the affirmative. The goal of pure science is to reduce the number of unknowns with which it has to deal to a minimum. Every step in this direction is a step in scientific progress, for in taking that step new relationships are disclosed, and the mind finds itself more and more clearly imaged in the mirror of Nature.

The New Physics has achieved a still more profound synthesis in the correlation it has effected between light or radiant energy and the electrical particles of which atoms are composed. Twentieth-century physics rests upon a conceptual basis that is utterly new in scientific thought. I refer to the Quantum Theory and Wave Mechanics. As laymen we cannot hope to follow the physicists very far into these new fields. The trail has been blazed, but only an experienced guide can follow the markings without getting lost in a maze of new and unfamiliar concepts.

Both Quantum Theory and Wave Mechanics grew out of necessities to explain facts of experiment for which the older physics had no explanation. The old road ended in a swamp of contradictions. For example, we all know that a black body gradually heated first gives out a dull red glow, which, as the temperature is increased, becomes more and more like the white light of the sun. In the language of physics, the distribution of energy in the spectrum of the radiation from a black body depends upon its temperature. The older physics, assuming that energy is radiated continuously from the vibrating atoms of a hot body, arrived at a relation between temperature and spectral distribution. This theoretical relation did not fit the facts of experiment. At the end of the last century, Max Planck made the revolutionary assumption that instead of energy being radiated in continuous waves it is emitted in atoms of energy, or *quanta.* That is to say, the radiant energy from a vibrating particle is not given out in electromagnetic waves continuously like water from a hose, but in separate units like bullets from a machine gun. The energy in each bullet or quantum is equal to a constant h times the frequency of vibration. The formula between temperature and spectral distribution derived on this assumption *did* fit the facts. What this amounts to is that radiant energy behaves as if it consisted of *particles* of energy.

Equally hard for the wave conception are the facts of photoelectricity. When light of sufficiently short wave lengths falls on a metal plate, electrons are emitted from the plate. On the wave theory, the energy imparted to these electrons should vary with the intensity of the light. But it doesn't. The *number* of electrons emitted does so vary, but the *energy* of the individual electron depends upon the frequency of light, the higher the frequency, i.e., the shorter the wave length, the greater the energy with which the electron leaves the surface of the metal. It took quite a while and a great deal of careful investigation, but finally Robert Millikan and others succeeded in proving to the satisfaction of all physicists that the energy which light gives to the electron in the photoelectric effect is proportional to the frequency and that the constant factor of proportionality involves the same h which Planck had discovered in his study of the radiation from a black body. In other words, when energy is delivered by an electron to space as radiation, or when radiation imparts energy to an electron in the photoelectric effect, the transfer is made in standard packages E, equal to Planck's constant h times the frequency of the radiation. It was Einstein who, in 1905, offered the explanation that the energy of light waves, instead of being uniformly distributed over the wave front, is concentrated in localized bits or quanta, and that in any reaction between light and a material body the transaction is made in whole units, never fractions, of these quanta. Like matter and electricity, light and all forms of radiant energy are corpuscular. Some twenty years later Arthur Compton showed that when a light quantum, now called a photon, strikes an electron, there is a distribution of energy and momentum between the two, just as when two billiard balls collide. (The phenomenon is by no means as simple as this statement would make it seem, since in the case of photons energy change is shown as a change in frequency or wave length. But this interpretation of the "Compton effect" is universally accepted by the New Physicists.)

This conception of light as particles of energy is fundamental in Quantum Theory. But the facts on which the older wave theory of light was formulated, facts which temporarily at least seemed to disprove Sir Isaac Newton's conception of light as corpuscles, these facts still remain. That two beams of light, originating from the same source and traveling by paths of slightly different lengths to the same point on a screen, may conspire to produce alternate regions of light and darkness is easily explained if we think of light as waves. It is easily demonstrated in the case of sound waves and water waves. At those points where two trains of waves from a common source arrive in opposite phase, crest to trough, compression to rarefaction, the result is darkness in the case of light, silence in the case of sound—the well-known phenomenon of interference in wave theory. But the phenomenon makes hard going for the particle conception of light. It is not easy to see how two bullets from a machine gun can arrive at the same point at the same time and produce the same effect as no bullet. This was a particularly bad stretch for the trail blazers of the New Physics. Conceptually, it is really not easy going even for the physicist today. As for the naive mind of the layman—well, his faith in the superior insight of the physicist has to carry him over the next long step which the New Physics took. That step consisted in accepting the apparently contradictory notions of light as both waves and/or particles of energy. But the step was worth the effort, for it led to a further synthesis in our conception of the nature of the physical universe more far-reaching than any that had hitherto been taken.

One may state that synthesis very briefly and in broad terms simply by saying that the ultimate stuff of all physical reality exhibits itself always in the dual aspect of waves and particles. This amounts to saying that whether we are thinking of the reality back of the phenomena of radiation, the electromagnetic waves of radio, light, X-rays—or of the electrons, protons, neutrons of which the atoms are built, we may expect to find, if we push the analysis far enough, something that must be conceived of as possessing this dual nature. Wave Mechanics is the branch of the New Physics that treats of phenomena from this point of view. It would be hard to ascribe the parts played by pure mathematics on the one hand and experimental physics on the other in the evolution of this new product of human thought. So intimately correlated are the contributions from both fields that one has the feeling that here is the product of a supermind finding expression in the thought and activities of scores of separate minds. However that may be, the notion of the wave-particle character of light, hitherto known only as electromagnetic waves, suggested the possibility to both mathematicians and physicists that electrons, thus far known only as particles, might also be leading a double life. To the Frenchman De Broglie is usually credited the honor of having first advanced the idea in definite and mathematically formulated terms, but Schroedinger in Austria developed it into a fairly complete mathematical theory, based on the fundamental idea that the dynamics of material and electrical particles can be mathematically described in terms and relationships that also apply to waves.

In 1927 Davison and Germer in America and G. P. Thomson independently in England showed experimentally that when a beam of swiftly moving electrons is reflected from or passes through a very thin film of a crystal, the uniformly spaced atoms of the crystal diffract the electrons in exactly the same manner as crystals diffract X-rays, or as the uniform spacings of a diffraction grating diffract visible light. This fact can be most easily explained by ascribing exactly the same wave-like properties to electrons as are possessed by light. Today we have the "electron microscope" in which the wave characteristics of electrons play the same role as do light waves in the ordinary microscope.

Thus we find, in our conception of the electron, the same duality of wave and particle aspect as confronts us in thinking of light. It is the wave aspect of light with which we are most familiar, while in the case of the electron the situation is just the reverse. But we have not reached the end of the unification brought about by Quantum Theory and Wave Mechanics. We have spoken of the "mass of the electron" and its electric charge. The mental picture is that of a tiny bit of something solid somehow carrying about with it another unknown something, its electric charge. The mental picture of the photon, the light unit, is of a localized bit of energy in a wave. There is no suggestion of anything solid or material in this latter picture. But in the Compton effect and in the fact that light rays are affected by a gravitational field, there rests the implication of something like a particle. What if any is the difference between the energy divorced from matter in radiation and energy associated with matter in the free electron? The answer of a thoroughgoing New Physicist is that there is no difference. The first is the energy of light waves localized in photons, the energy of each photon being the product of the universal constant h and the vibration frequency of the light wave. The energy of the electron is likewise the energy of waves, the waves that are the wave aspect of the electron itself.

And this brings us to that profound synthesis effected by the mathematical mind of Albert Einstein as a necessary consequence of the theory of Relativity. This synthesis is stated in that very simple but completely revolutionary mathematical relationship, $E=mc^2$, which is the famous "Einstein Equation"—the theoretical basis of the vast scientific and technological development that released the energy of the atom in the destructive power of the atom bomb. In the form given, the Einstein equation states that the energy equivalent measured in ergs of 1 gram of matter (about 1/28 of an ounce) is equal to the square of the velocity of light measured in centimeters per second, or 9×10^{20} (9 followed by 20 ciphers). This can be stated in the more familiar terms, kilowatt hours, that appear on our electric light bills. In these units the energy equivalent of one gram of matter is 25,000,000 kilowatt hours. A 100-watt light bulb dissipates only one-tenth of a kilowatt of power so that our one gram of matter represents enough energy to light 250 million 100-watt lamps for one hour. If this amount of energy were all released in one second the illumination produced during that second would be 3600 times 250,000,000 or 9 trillion times that of our 100-watt lamp.

Put into mechanical terms this amount of energy is the equivalent of the work done by some 33 millions of horses working for one hour. Its destructive effect, if released all at once, would be the same as that produced by the impact of a 32 million ton weight dropped from a height of 1000 feet.

In the Smythe Report on Atomic Energy we are told that "one kilogram of matter, if converted entirely into energy, would give 25 billion kilowatt hours of energy" equal to the total energy output of the electric power industry in the United States for a period of two months. The burning of one kilogram of coal will produce 8.5 kilowatt hours.

To the layman these figures are fantastic, but the devastation wrought by the atom bomb at Hiroshima and Nagasaki leaves no room for doubt of the awful truth of the innocent-looking equation, $E=mc^2$.

Thus the ultimate stuff of the so-called inert matter of traditional physics has come to be recognized as tremendously concentrated bits of energy, wave packets, composed of waves whose vibration frequencies are as much greater than those of ordinary light as these frequencies are greater than the frequencies of sound waves. Conservation of energy and conservation of matter, the two great generalizations of nineteenth-century physics, have been reduced to a single principle, the conservation of energy. The universe of stars and atoms, of matter and radiation, all of nature animate and inanimate, including the brain cells of the scientist and the philosopher, are, in the view of the New Physics, but particularized expressions of the energy which *is* the material universe. Physical science has resolved the problem of the "one and the many" to the more definite problem of the two aspects of the primordial energy of the cosmos itself, namely waves and particles.

In the opening paragraph of his *Nature of the Physical World*[3] Sir Arthur Eddington whimsically speaks of the two tables on which he writes—the table which to common sense is simply a table and nothing more, a hard fixed, fairly permanent unit of experience, adequately described by the term "a table". But when, as a scientist familiar with the modern ideas of the nature of matter, he considers the ultimate reality back of that bit of sense experience, he finds it undergoing a fantastic metamorphosis. What his senses tell him is a simple solid object, sharply defined with reference to other objects, quite distinct from that which is "not table," becomes something quite different. In the light of his scientific knowledge it is transformed, as by magic, into a swarm of non-substantial electrons, protons, neutrons, and their still less substantial fields of electric and magnetic force. The sharp dividing line between "table" and "not table" fades into a penumbral region, at no precise point of which one can say "table" ends and "not table" begins.

When, in spite of common sense, we have brought ourselves to think with Sir Arthur of the scientific table as a swarm of very energetic particles, each carrying its bit of a mysterious something called electricity, and in the aggregate occupying but by no means filling the space which the common sense table seems to occupy, we are told that this is far too substantial a picture to fit the scientific facts. The electric particles are nothing much in and of themselves. The reality of each particle rests largely in its "field of force," and this field of force reveals itself in the power which the

3 *Nature of the Physical World,* Macmillan, New York, 1929.

particle has to affect other particles, a sort of center, so to speak, with no definite circumference.

But just as we are about ready to visualize the ultimate particles as geometrical points, we are told that this is far from the case. The electrons, protons and neutrons must be conceived of as wave packets, which cannot strictly be said to have any definite position in space at any specified time. Due to its wave aspect, the position of the electron as a particle can be specified only within a certain range of probabilities. There is a sense in which each electron may be said to occupy the whole of space. What this amounts to is that, due to its wave aspect, the electron does not exist as an individual, but only in its relation to other electrons, or protons, and their fields of force. The individualized material or electrical particles have, for the New Physicist, ceased to exist, and in their places are highly energized portions of the space-time continuum. The nature of this energy is what in gross experience we call vibratory, a to and fro movement in space *and* time. In the New Physics it is conceived only as certain mathematical relations in Wave Mechanics. Just as in Relativity, the ether with its electromagnetic and gravitational fields is resolved into relationships in a world of pure thought, so in Wave Mechanics the world of seemingly solid tangible reality appears in its last analysis as a universe whose cosmic substance is one primordial energy that transcends all human powers of imagery. We can know it in the relationships that can only be expressed in mathematical symbols.

Certainly we have come far from the common sense "table" in our quest with Sir Arthur of the physical reality back of sense experience. Proceeding in the direction of the microscopic from the gross material object to its molecules, thence to the atom and still further to the ultimate electrons, protons and neutrons, we arrive at a point beyond which the wave aspect of matter comes to predominate over the particle aspect and the Newtonian abstraction of a *material particle* has to give place to that other abstraction of *energy*. Thus the two unknowns, matter and energy of the classical physics, are reduced to a single unknown *Energy*. In the earlier view, energy was thought of as the cause of the changes in matter conceived of as inert. In the later view the *inertness* of *matter* is but a mask which conceals tremendous concentrations of energy. Astronomers tell us that the radiant energy of the stars originates in subatomic changes in which an infinitesimal part of the inherent energy of the stellar atoms is converted into light.

In this new outlook, the Mover and that which is moved are One. The universe, *perceived* as many, must be *conceived* as one, and for the finite human mind that unity must and can only be apprehended, in the symbolic terms of mathematical relationships. Back of the chaos of the countless forms of material objects, the infinite variety of chemical substances, lie the simple numerical relations of the atomic numbers. Radiation, from the electromagnetic waves of radiotelephony, through the glories of sunset hues, down to the mystery of the cosmic rays, is but a continuous series of numbers—vibration frequencies. Search far enough for the basis of that which underlies our sense experiences, which we think of as coming from an outer world, and we find only this outstanding fact, the mathematical relatedness between the measurable aspects of all phenomena.

Naturally we raise the question: "Why should this be true?" Why, when physical science has gone as far as it can go along any one line of its quest of the ultimate nature of things, should it find at the end only mathematical relatedness? There are two answers to the questions. I suspect that our acceptance of one or the other of these answers will be largely a matter of our own individual psychology. The first answer seems obvious enough and superficially satisfying. It runs something like this: Measurement is the road by which physical science travels to the understanding of phenomena. Measurement always results in numerical quantities. Number is the basis of mathematical analysis, therefore the only goal that can be reached along this road is mathematical relationships. This answer seems conclusive enough. Physical science creates its image world by confining itself to the quantitative elements of physical events. Since all else is excluded from its "universe of discourse," it follows of necessity that nothing save mathematical relationships can possibly appear in that image world.

But there is a further question of tremendous significance which this answer ignores. Why or how does it happen that this process of analysis carried along different lines leads, as it has led in the history of science, to a constantly increasing unification of our concepts of the ultimate reality back of all phenomena? The mathematical relations of Maxwell's equations synthesized the phenomena of electromagnetism and of light. Einstein's analysis of the concepts of time and space led to a synthesis of electromagnetism and gravitation in his four-dimensional space-time continuum. The emission and absorption of radiation, the phenomena of thermionics, photoelectricity, radioactivity, the bewildering complexities of atomic structure and atomic spectra, the relatedness of the chemical properties of the elements and the identity of matter and energy, are all bound together in the symbolic representations of the Quantum Theory and Wave Mechanics. Are these all the results of happy chance that has befallen man in his search for the answer to the riddle of the universe? Finally, is the abiding faith in the unity of nature, which is the driving force behind all scientific endeavor—is this simply an *ignis fatuus* that lures the human spirit always further into the swamp of the eternally unknowable?

The second answer to the question takes account of all these by saying that there is an intimate correlation between the structure of the physical universe and the structure of the human mind. That which is behind the world of sense experience is in its essence closely akin to that mysterious something which in each of us moves in the realm of thought, the thinking self. The image world of science is not a creation of the finite mind of man. It is rather a real image, real though still blurred and distorted, of the absolute reality that is the Mind of the universe.

The acceptance of this second answer may well be characterized as an act of religious faith, but as we have tried to point out at the end of the previous chapter, a faith that requires no sacrifice of reason. Rather, it is a faith that gives point and meaning to the scientific quest, a faith that gives a rational basis for what must otherwise be deemed nothing more than an irrational urge of the human spirit—the instinctive desire to *know*, the expression in civilized man of the primitive instinct of curiosity. How foolish would be the quest of truth if at the end one expects to find only one sublime delusion in which all lesser delusions are merged!

In following the New Physics in its search for the ultimate nature of matter, we have arrived at the conception of the whole material universe, from nebulae to electrons, as reducible to a universal something called *energy*, whose nature is unknown except as it is symbolized in mathematical relationships. Going back to the older physics with its abstraction of matter as inert, "tranquil and devoid of action," and of energy as that which is "capable of producing effect," we find that it is the latter which has survived the synthesis of the New Physics. Matter conceived of as inert has given place to relatively stable concentrations of energy, and instead of a physical universe of material particles, passive save as they are affected by transfers of energy, we must envision a world in which the "capacity for producing effects" is inherent in the very stuff and substance of all that we call physical. No dead world this, originally endowed with an initial store of energy which it must ultimately dissipate under the inescapable second law of thermodynamics; not a machine, wound up somehow in the past, doomed to run down sometime in the future. Rather do we find ourselves part of a world of restless pulsating energy, an energy which in its outer aspects reveals itself to our senses as the solid earth, the unresting sea, the moving air, and the light of the stars, while in its inner aspect its unity finds expression in the magic of numbers and in the symbolic language of mathematics. As Sir James Jeans has put it: "The world (as we can know it) is more like a great *thought* than a great *thing*." The New Physics presents the Universal Mind, the expression of whose thought is the physical world, not only as the passive contemplative mind, the matrix of the mathematical realities symbolized in Relativity, but as the creative mind endowed with "infinite capacity for producing effects." We take only a small step when we pass from the universal Energy of modern science to God, the Creator, who said "Let there be light."

I think we take no longer step when we identify the rational element of the human mind with the rational Mind of the Universe and the creative power of human thought with the creative energy which is the physical world. Considered as a physical object, man's body is composed of electrons, protons, neutrons—locally energized regions of the cosmos itself. The inner aspect of the assembly of "wave packets," oriented and correlated so as to function as a living organism, is consciousness—a property hitherto assigned solely to the brain and the nervous system, but in the later view inhering in the whole physical organism. Is it a wild plunge of sheer speculation to suppose that, just as the human body is a localized expression of the cosmic Energy, so the human mind is an individualized expression of the cosmic Mind? Just as we must think of the electron not as an individual discrete particle existing in and of itself but by virtue of its wave characteristics and its field of force existing as an integral part of the whole physical universe, may we not also think of individual consciousness not as separate and apart but as integrated with that Universal Mind whose thought is the ultimate reality that lies back of all phenomena?

Now one is aware that in such a synthesis there is nothing that is scientifically valuable, at least not for our Western minds steeped in a philosophy based on the assumptions of the uniqueness of personality and the dualism of mind and matter. One is also aware that it is not particularly novel. It is inherent in Platonism and in all philosophic thought of the idealistic school. Its special significance, I think, lies in the fact that it comes not as a product of a system of metaphysical rationalizations, but as an easy, even if not necessary, implication of an intellectual movement whose initial premises involved the independent objective existence of material bodies and the complete dualism of mind and matter. Classical physics cast the scientist in the passive role of the observer, independent of and quite apart from what is observed. Modern physics finds that the mere act of observation has an effect upon the physical event. The world we know is physically altered by the process of our knowing it. The observer is of necessity and in a very real sense a part of that which is observed.

While it is true that what may well be called the religious implications of the new world-view given by modern physics are without scientific significance, I feel very sure that they are of tremendous practical import to the thoughtful mind. In these latter years the scientist has, in the mind of the layman, taken over the rôle of priest and prophet. The voice of science has come to assume an authority which for earlier generations was ascribed to the voice of God in the teachings of the Scriptures and of the Church. The evidence of this change of attitude is found in the multitude of books that have appeared in recent years from the leaders of science for the purpose of bringing to the nonscientific world the new views of the nature of the physical universe. The atomistic mechanism of the last century, backed by the prestige of its vast material achievements, presented a world-view of complete mechanical determinism against which all human striving appeared only as an insignificant phase of the downhill tendency of a cosmos doomed to the ultimate stagnation of complete thermodynamic equilibrium. The origin of life and the whole process of organic evolution was but an evanescent ripple upon the surface of the stream of cosmic disintegration. The best that science had to offer in response to the human cry "What is it all about?" was the counsel of an attitude of philosophic stoicism or one of enlightened hedonism. It would seem probable that the decline of faith in the teachings of traditional religion, the increasing moral chaos, the growing tendency to accept the pleasure principle as the guide to personal conduct, and the breakdown of all ethical standards in international relationships, all find a certain degree of explanation in the negative attitude of mind with regard to the cosmic significance of human values engendered by this earlier scientific world-view. Let me hasten to add that there is no desire to place responsibility for the present troubled state of human affairs upon the shoulders of science. Such a charge could not stand any more than the charge that religion should bear the onus of the bigotry, cruelty and persecutions that have been the expressions of human intolerance in the spiritual evolution of man. All that is implied is that any system of thought that leads to a denial of the possibility of human freedom, that reduces conduct to the status of the inevitable response to external stimuli, and that denies the operation of a creative principle in the spiritual aspirations of the human species must result in an atmosphere of pessimism in which moral values wither and the spirit loses that sense of its own essential worth without which all that is intrinsically human in man must perish.

We have spoken of the "freedom of man" as though something in the new scientific view ran counter to the concept of complete physical causation implicit in the older physics. This raises the question as to whether this is true and whether the future behavior of electrons and protons is in any less degree determined by their present state than was assumed with regard to the chemical atoms of nineteenth-century physics.

Does the fact that the nerves and brain and all the cells of the human body are reducible by physical analysis to nonmaterial wave-particle elements allow any possibility that the activity of that body as a living organism is in any less degree determined by the physical laws which govern the movements and relations of these elements than would be the case if they were the chemical atoms of classical physics? In short, does the New Physics offer any more ground for belief in the possibility of the operation of effective purpose in nature, of which man is a part, than did atomistic mechanism?

In the answers which the great minds of modern science give to this question we find the same sharp line of cleavage which attempts to answer it have always developed. It would almost seem that the choice between freedom and determinism arises from some inherent quality of the individual's mind. The problem is as old as the history of human thought. Strictly speaking it does not come within the realm of physical science. It belongs to the philosophical task of interpretation.

The man of science must occupy an equivocal position. As an experimentalist, he assumes that nature behaves according to immutable laws and that all elements of chance or purpose must be eliminated from the conditions of his experiments. At the same time he recognizes the effectiveness of his own purpose in choosing one line of investigation in preference to another, or in choosing to investigate at all. Thus he acts on two contradictory assumptions, and gets along perfectly well so long as he *acts* and leaves the logic of his behavior to the philosophers to worry about.

But the implications of the problem go much deeper than the question of whether man is a free agent or an automaton. It involves the much broader question of whether the world image, as formed by the finite mirror of human understanding, is to be conceived of as a predetermined pattern eternally existent in the Mind of the Universe, as are the individual pictures on a motion picture film, which, projected on the screen of human experience, create the illusion of an evolutionary process. Or are we to think of the world, as we must know it through the limitations of our senses, as thought and purpose in the infinite Mind that can only find full expression through our free participation as actors in the drama of existence? This reduces itself for the individual to the very practical question of whether or not he has within himself an effective power of fashioning the pattern of his individual world. For society as a whole it becomes the question as to what, if any, power resides in man in the aggregate to control those vast social forces of which he is at once both the creator and the victim.

While the New Physics does not solve the age-old problem, yet it does throw a far different light upon it from that which pure mechanism affords. The determinism inherent in the older conception of inert atoms whose motions are conditioned by purely physical laws arises from the unproved assumption that those laws, experimentally proven in the case of gross material bodies, apply with mathematical precision to the atoms themselves. On this assumption, and since all matter including that of brain cells is composed of these atoms, there can be no element of uncertainty in the sequence of events in the material world. In short, determinism is implicit in the fundamental conceptions of the older physics. The order of the world is established like the sequence of the individual frames of the motion picture film, and the life of the individual and the course of human history are predetermined by the blind impersonal forces that control the movements of the atoms.

The dual aspect of waves and particles in which the ultimate stuff of the physical world presents itself, however, necessitates a radical revision in our thinking on this question of fate versus freedom. In an earlier chapter we suggested a psychical as well as a physical quality in matter in order to account for the purposive coordination that appears in living organisms. Even so, under the older mechanistic view we are still faced with the problem of just when or where or how the psychical can have any effective influence on the sequence of physical events. Obviously we have simply carried the mind-matter problem down to the atomic level.

Simply to endow the chemical atom with an esoteric psychical property doesn't free it from the necessity that chemical and physical laws impose on its behavior. If *purpose* is to find expression in the control of the sequence of physical events, then there must be somewhere a break in that chain of causation which makes a future state the uniquely necessary result of a present state.

Just such a break occurs as a result of the wave-particle nature of the subatomic constituents of the atoms and of radiation. Conceived as a particle, the electron at any moent may be thought of as having a definite position in space and an equally definite magnitude and direction of its velocity. As a particle, in the old sense, these coordinates are enough to determine its position and velocity at the next succeeding moment. As a wave-particle, however, there is an inherent uncertainty in the simultaneous determination of both its position and momentum. This uncertainty makes the immediate future of the electron a matter of probability rather than of mathematical certainty. Within the limits of that probability the future of the individual electron, proton or neutron is not completely determined. In other words the wave-particle has in the passage from present to future a measure of *freedom*.

If now, as we have proposed, the stuff of the world is both physical and psychical, then we may reasonably suppose that within this region of *physical* uncertainty the *psychical* may operate as an effective agent in controlling the course of events for the individual wave-particle. When we say that the future of an individual electron is uncertain, we must mean, I think, that the future state is a matter either of chance or choice. To assume the former is to imply the possibility of the latter.

When we speak of a nonphysical element involved in the nature of electrons and protons as *psychical,* all that we meant to imply was a certain potentiality of response to future as well as to past events. This, as we have seen, is a characteristic of the behavior of the matter constituting an organism. In conscious experience it gives rise to a sense of freedom to initiate movements directed to some future end. What we have said then is that in the ultimate particles of the stuff of the physical world there is inherent that quality by which we account for the purposive behavior of living organisms, and which is an element of our own conscious experience. It follows therefore that if there is such a thing as conscious purpose in the universe, that purpose can find expression in material forms and patterns and in coordinated activities whose external aspect can be accounted for in physical terms, but whose organizing principle lies outside the categories of matter and energy, and this expression of conscious purpose can be effected by a process that is no more and no less inexplicable than the movement of a finger as an act of conscious will.

The cognitive Mind of the universe was postulated as a basis for our acceptance of the objective existence of the mathematical relations of Relativity theory. The fact that the ultimate elements of both matter and radiant energy possess the properties of both waves and particles, allows at least, even though it may not necessitate, the acceptance of the idea of the effective operation in the physical world of that which in conscious experience we call *purpose.* Relativity leads us to the conception of the universe of space-time and the mathematical realities of field physics as a great Thought. Quantum Theory and Wave Mechanics allow us to believe in the operations of external nature as the expression of a great Purpose.

And what of individual freedom in the world-view of the New Science in which *mind* and *energy* have supplanted "the atom and the void" of atomistic mechanism? What I think we must say is that the problem still remains outside the domain of objective science. The human individual, like the electrons and protons of which his mind and body are constituted, appears in a dual role. As an organism he responds to physical and chemical stimuli with a uniformity that makes the probability of much of his behavior a practical certainty. As a group, he seeks pleasure and avoids pain, chooses companionship rather than solitude, prefers life to death. As an individual, he may make just the opposite choices. Even as an organism he presents wide individual variations from the statistical norm. "One man's meat may be another man's poison." A super-mind, observing human behavior in the aggregate, would undoubtedly describe it in general, mathematical laws exactly as the scientist describes the behavior of large numbers of electrons, protons and neutrons. But if this super-mind carried his observation to the behavior of the individual, he would certainly have to set up an "Uncertainty Principle" which would allow a latitude for the operation of chance or purpose. This, it would seem, is as far as the New Physics goes in resolving the age-old dilemma of fate and freedom, and this, I think, is no mean distance. It does not give positive evidence in favor of freedom, but by replacing the bond of mathematical certainty between the present and the future, by the flexible tie of statistical probability, it makes freedom a scientifically plausible hypothesis instead of a scientific impossibility.

In the newer view the origin of life and the vast scheme of organic evolution do not appear as a meaningless episode, a spark in a dying world, but rather as the expression of a cosmic "will to live" in a universe surcharged with the potentialities of life.

The older world-view of science was but a phase in the slow process of the evolution of human thought. The essence of the experimental search for truth lies in approaching reality from the impersonal, objective point of view. The observer must of necessity assume a perfectly passive role, demanding of his own intellectual function of interpretation the same detached objective certitude that he demands of the physical instruments of his experiments. It is entirely natural that the scientific movement begun by Galileo and Newton should lead to a philosophy of mechanistic determinism. This was the price that man had to pay for his eating of the fruit of the tree of scientific knowledge. In the same breath, it is to be said to the lasting glory of science that the will to know did not stop at a point that left "man the unknown" alone in a dead world of physical causation. In its latest development physical science has led to the conception of a potentially living world replete with energy, in which biological evolution as we know it on our earth is but one link in a universal evolutionary process, the bare outlines of which we are beginning to see—an evolution extending from the minuscular world of the subatomic to the myriad stars of our galaxy, and thence to the millions of nebulae dwelling in the vast reaches of cosmic space. As when one drops a photographic plate into the developer and sees appearing in the red light of the dark room the first faint vague shadows of what will become the sharp, clear image of the finished picture, so science today is revealing the image (still latent in human understanding) in the Mind of God, of a world of spiritual reality—a world in which the driving, restless inquiring spirit of man finds itself as a finite expression of the infinite Spirit that moves upon the "face of the deep".

Chapter 7

The Inner World of Psychology

"Now the processes involved in the production of works of science and of art are life processes occurring within men —The origin of each finding of science and of each work of art is the experience of a man."

William Lowe Bryan[1]

"It is through dynamic psychology that we can for the first time understand the emotional inhibitions and distortions which have always prevented men from translating religious ideals into actualities."

Joshua Loth Liebman[2]

In the preceding chapters we have tried to trace the development of the conceptual background of physical science from that of atomistic mechanism in a pluralistic world as set forth by Newton, through successive stages of unification to the modern view that reduces all physical reality to the status of mathematical relationships and all becoming to the expression of a primordial energy which is potentially, at least, susceptible to the operation of nonphysical influence. We have taken the position that in this new world-view the ultimate stuff of mind and the ultimate stuff of matter are in essence but two aspects of the same reality.

Against this new background, the conception of matter as intrinsically inert and lifeless gives place to that of energy with its creative potentialities, and mechanistic determinism is succeeded by statistical laws in which probabilities sup-

1 *Wars of Families of Minds*: Yale University Press, 1940.

2 *Peace of Mind*: Simon and Schuster, 1946.

plant mathematical certainty in the passage from present to future.

Physical science has thus achieved a marvelous synthesis in the conceptual basis of the world of phenomena and the world of mental realities, a synthesis in which the acceptance of a Universal Mind is implicit. We speak of this Mind as a unity. But what of that individualized unit of consciousness which for each of us is solitary and separate, the self which stands alone in a world which is not-self? Does it not occupy the unique position of subject to which all else, all other individual minds, even the Mind of the Universe, bear the relation of object? Is not the fact of one's own individual independent existence separate and apart from everything else in the world of thought and the world of things the one ultimate certainty in all experience? One can accept as an intellectual proposition the notion of a world of matter and energy that, in the mind of God, is fused into a unity of mental reality. But outside this world, viewing it as an object of consciousness, stands the conscious thinking self, the "I" which exists independent of and apart from all other existences.

Thus speaks the self-conscious individualism of modern Western mind. For that mind there is no bridging the gulf that separates the Ego from the Cosmos. I speak of *my* hands, *my* feet, *my* brain cells, *my* thoughts, *my* emotions, and the use of the first person possessive pronoun implies an unresolved dualism, a possessor and something possessed. Science may present us with a solution in the "riddle of the physical universe," but in that solution there is no symbol that stands for the deepest mystery in all this mysterious world, the mystery of the individual conscious questioning spirit of man. "Men are but cells within a mighty brain," is a poet's conception, but for our modern Western psychology, this is a poet's fancy rather than a statement of fact. For our every day common sense, there is no recognition of organic unity between what goes on in our individual minds and what transpires outside of them.

For the Eastern mind the quest of reality lies along the road of contemplation. The key to the riddle of all being lies within consciousness. The goal of all seeking is "recognition," the identification of the self with the soul of the world; the reward of the quest is the freeing of the self from all striving and its rest in the eternal impersonal oneness of the universe. The testimony of the senses is deceptive. Empirical knowledge leads only to delusion. Therefore the road to recognition starts with the denial of the independent existence of any reality back of sense impression and ends with the mystic experience of the union of the individual soul with the soul of all in Nirvana.

This is the solution of the problem to which centuries of contemplation have led the ancient mind of the East—a negative sort of solution for the modern mind of the West. For us meditation, contemplation, the renunciation of desire and the quest of a mystic experience that can never be attained until all striving to attain it has ceased is paradoxical to the point of absurdity. So far as what we call practical results are concerned, one might as well give up and go fishing. The end results are the same and it is far simpler and easier. We point with pride to the material products of Western Civilization, skyscrapers, the radio, the automobile, air conditioning, mass production, airplanes, battleships, submarines, high explosives, and the thousand-and-one agencies both for enhancing life and for spreading destruction and death. We contrast all this with what in our eyes is the stagnation and decay of the declining civilizations of India and China, and we feel assured that pragmatically, at least, the ancient thought of the East leads nowhere in the evolution of the human species. Of what avail is it, we ask, that a saint or a sage here and there arrives at an ineffable state of consciousness which can find no expression in language or symbols, and has no meaning outside his individual mind, while the teeming millions about him spawn and suffer and die even as the beasts which perish? Truly, "East is East, and West is West, and never the twain shall meet."

However strange the mystic approach of the Eastern mind to reality may seem to us, conditioned as we are by centuries of individualism, it must be admitted that both the philosophic and religious thought of Western Civilization have been colored in no small measure by the infiltration of the thought of the Eastern Aryans. In the days long before the virile spirit of the Greeks found expression in the aesthetics and metaphysics of Grecian culture, Hindu civilization and Hindu thought were old. The seeds of this ancient culture were carried by traders, emissaries and missionaries into the fertile soil of Greek thought. Scholars are agreed that from very early times the two branches of the Aryan family were in contact with each other, and it may well be inferred that the mystic cult of Pythagoras was the Greek version of Hindu mysticism and asceticism. Thus the philosophy of Plato, who was an admirer of Pythagoras, and of his belief in the mathematical order of the world, may in many of its essentials be traced to Hindu origin. Plato's deprecation of the testimony of the senses as illusory and unreliable, his emphasis upon the ephemeral and transient nature of physical phenomena, and his insistence upon the ascendancy of reason, are the imprint of the active Greek mind upon the passive conceptions coming from Hindu thought. Platonism in turn was incorporated in the ethical and metaphysical teaching of the early Christian fathers, who carried the Platonic notion of the primacy of the soul to a denial of the claims of the body and taught asceticism as a means of realization of the union of the soul with God. Out of these teachings grew monasticism and celibacy as necessary steps on the road to salvation. Puritanism was the Protestant expression of this same trend.

We note, however, in the Western mystical conception a certain deep-seated difference from the idea as it exists in Eastern thought. In both the spirit is reality and the body is illusion. Yet all through Western teaching, the soul is conceived of as a unity in and of itself, separate and distinct from another independent entity, God, the absolute soul of all. The individual soul of man is, to use a chemical analogy, an atom of consciousness associated with an individual organism. The figure most commonly employed is to characterize man in his spiritual essence as a "child of God." There is no sort of identification. The goal of all spiritual striving is communion of the soul with God. In the Oriental mind this very sense of individual isolation of the self as a distinct and separate existence is the supreme illusion. Salvation is recognition, the freeing of the soul from the sense of its separateness and its fusion with the impersonal, eternal, changeless soul of all things. Hence salvation is not to be achieved through struggle but through resignation. Not the development of the individual's spiritual powers, but the loss of all desire and will, the complete submersion of the illusory individual self in the Absolute — this, in Eastern thought, is the soul's true quest.

It is obvious, I think, that neither of these views of the nature of the individual mind conforms to the world-view of modern objective science. As a matter of fact, following the scientific awakening of the seventeenth century, physical science did not concern itself in any considerable degree with this problem which has always been at the heart of all metaphysical speculation. As we have seen, the experimental method came as a reaction against the speculative, religio-philosophic, preoccupation of Scholasticism.

In its role as observer of the events in an external world, the scientific mind has no need to inquire as to its own nature. To quote Tobias Dantzig's paraphrase of the wisdom of Solomon, "Let us hear the conclusion of the matter: Read your instruments, and obey mathematics; for this is the whole duty of the scientist." For most men of science the metaphysical speculations of the logicians and philosophers are so much logic-chopping and verbal hair-splitting on matters which are beyond the reach of the scientific method, and hence of no immediate concern to them as scientists. Psychology, the study of the nature and operation of the human mind, was consigned to the philosophers and the theologians.

It was inevitable, however, that the success of the experimental method in the field of external reality should ultimately lead to attempts to apply it in the realm of the mind. Why not subject "the observer" to his own experimental technique, make his mental operations the field of the same sort of objective investigation as he applies to physical phenomena? Now one recognizes at once that there are certain inherent difficulties in carrying out this program due to the fact that externalization of psychological phenomena is in the very nature of things quite impossible. The roles of both "observer" and "observed" have to be played by the same actor, and the rapid shift from one role to the other is a disturbing factor that throws doubt on the scientific validity of the method. It is a great deal like trying to study the minute details of one's features by suddenly jumping behind the mirror in an attempt to seize one's own image.

Psychology as an independent discipline is scarcely a century old, even though many of its still unsolved problems occupied the attention of Plato and Aristotle and of all philosophers since their time. Two approaches to the study of the mind are possible. That from the inside, introspection, has been employed by philosophers from time immemorial. The method is purely observational, and involves the difficult and scientifically dangerous procedure of drawing conclusions from data that are not free from subjective influences. Each one of us carries about with him the equipment for this sort of psychological study, but we can never be sure that either the object or subject of the observation, namely the observation of mental processes by the mind itself, has anything more than individual significance. The study of one's own mental processes gives one no scientific basis for assuming that one is thereby gaining knowledge of the mental processes of others. One may by the introspective method arrive at the firm conviction that one's own power of choice is free and not determined by external factors. There is, however, absolutely no warrant for concluding that another individual using the same method would reach the same conviction. The very fact that for centuries this has been a battle ground of philosophers implies that by this technique we are quite unable to reach conclusions that carry the weight of the scientific certainty that inheres in physical laws.

The observational technique may be extended to the behavior of other individuals. Knowledge of mental states in another is inferred on the assumption that the same behavior on the part of two individuals is accompanied by the same mental state in each. The observer is thus thrown back on his own immediate awareness of the mental states that exist in his own experience when his behavior is the same as that exhibited by another. It is apparent that when the psychologist draws any conclusion as to conscious experience of an experimental subject from the observable behavior of the subject, he has in fact to go back to the introspective technique, using his own immediately experienced correlation between mental state and behavior as the norm.

In experimental psychology the study of mental phenomena makes its claim to freedom from philosophy and to inclusion in the ranks of objective science. Quantitative data are obtained by the invention and use of indicating devices, aesthesiometers, tachistoscopes and chronoscopes, which provide means for the quantitative control of stimuli and the measurement of response. Sensation and perception are most amenable to investigation in this way. It is to be noted that the data so obtained do not in themselves have any necessary bearing on the conscious processes that accompany responses to stimuli, but are related rather to the train of physical and chemical changes that take place in the nervous system, initiated by the stimulus and ending in the specific response which the stimulus calls forth. The experimental technique as applied to sensation and perception is a study of the reactions of the physical organism to physical stimuli and should accordingly be classified as psycho-physics, rather than psychology. As an illustration, the well-known Weber-Fechner law, which perhaps is as close an approximation as psychology has ever attained to the scientific ideal of mathematical formulation of the results of psychological experiment, states facts that are pertinent to the nervous system as a whole rather than to mental processes *per se.* This law assigns a numerical measure to sensation, the unit of measure being the difference between two sensations of the same sort, one of which can barely be perceived as differing in intensity from the other. The numerical magnitude of the difference between two sensations A and B of the same sort is the number of these "threshold" differences which can be perceived as the stimulus is changed continuously from that which arouses sensation A to that which arouses B. The law states that for the sensation to increase in arithmetical progression, the stimulus must increase in geometrical progression. This introduces a mathematical conception into the description of a psychological process, but the relation finds its explanation in the physical aspects of nerve impulses rather than in any quantitative property pertaining to the conscious process of perception. Analysis will show that the quantitative relationship given by the law finds an explanation in purely physical terms without any reference at all to the conscious experience, or without invoking any quantitative property in that experience.

The case just cited is typical of all attempts by the experimental method to reduce mental processes to the operations of laws that can be formulated in mathematical terms. In every such case the investigator is dealing with the outer rather than the inner aspect of the conscious mind. Experimental psychology in its use of the objective methods of physics and chemistry is thus really the study of the behavior of the human organism as related to the brain and nervous system, and its search is for necessary and determined relationships in the sequence of events that originate in the stimulation of the sense organs and terminate in some form of observable behavior. Like his scientific model, the physicist, the experimental psychologist seeks to eliminate, or chooses to ignore, consciousness as a determining factor in this sequence. His ideal subject would be a robot with a human brain and nervous system, but without the disturbing influence of consciousness. Lacking this, he devises his experiments so as to minimize as far as possible the subjective element.

Experimental psychology had its origin in Germany. Its first and greatest exponent was Wilhelm Wundt (1832-1920). He was a student of Helmholtz, whom I prefer to class a physicist and physiologist rather than a psychologist. Wundt accepted the introspective method as the beginning of psychological study, but insisted upon experiment as an auxiliary means of acquiring knowledge of the mind. In 1879 he founded his psychological laboratory at Leipzig, where for the remaining years of his long life he worked with a zeal that few scientific men have surpassed. The Leipzig school became the center of the new movement which was to give psychology a place among the objective sciences. Students from all over the world came to acquire the technique of the new method, and to carry away with them the ideas which have in a large measure dominated psychological research and teaching up until very recent years. This has been particularly true in America, where many of the great names of the older generation in psychology are those of men who were trained at Leipzig. It is fair to say that, at the end of the nineteenth century, experimental psychology occupied a large part of the field of interest of psychologists, and that the assumptions implicit in the experimental approach colored their views as to the nature of the mind. Behavior is the only objective evidence we have of the operation of mental processes. Psychological experiments under controlled conditions show a certain measure of uniformity in the stimulus-response patterns, and the next step along the road of inference is that mental processes occur according to fixed laws. This leads to a psychological determinism quite analogous to that which the older physical science imposed upon external nature. So we find nineteenth-century psychology starting from the same premises and arriving at the same sort of conclusion as did the physical sciences, whose assumptions and methods it followed.

It is a matter of observation that these concepts have become an integral part of the world-view of many thoughtful men and women of this generation. Mechanistic determinism in the physical world finds its counterpart in the psychological determinism of Behaviorism. Man, a machine in a mechanical world, makes a self-consistent picture, which in these days of terrific social, political and moral upheaval seems to be as consonant as any with the chaotic moment in human history in which we find ourselves. Human conduct viewed in the large seems not to be the expression of the ordered purposes of rational self-directed individuals, but rather the inevitable irrational response of a highly organized animal to the dark and ominous forces inherent in the world and in himself.

The work of the twentieth-century exponents of the experimental method has done much to strengthen in present day thought this conception of physiologists and psychologists who come under the general, somewhat indefinite designation of "behaviorists". The extreme behavioristic view may be quoted from J. B. Watson, the most radical exponent of this school of psychologists. He says, "It is possible to write a psychology, to define it as the 'science of behavior', and never go back on the definition; never to use the terms consciousness, mental states, mind, content, will, and the like."[3]

Obviously this definition eliminates from the psychologist's "universe of discourse", most of those elements with which introspective psychology had concerned itself. It is to be assumed that since psychology in its generally accepted meaning is the science of the mind, the definition also excludes these elements from *mind*. Watson would transform the conscious individual into a mindless robot with a brain and nervous system, the ideal subject for the application of the experimental method.

It is pertinent to remark that the behaviorists generally have approximated this ideal by conducting their experiments on animals and very young children. Animal psychology must of necessity get along without the introspective technique, but it seems obvious enough that, if the results of the study of animal behavior are to be considered as anything more than descriptive, then the psychologist must call upon his own conscious experience in order to correlate in any fashion the observed facts. For example, one opens at random that delightful account of the behavior of our anthropoid cousins in Wolfgang Köhler's *The Mentality of Apes* and finds the following: "If under the pressure of necessity some special method, say of the use of tools, has been evolved (by the ape), one can confidently expect to find this new knowledge shortly utilized in 'play' where it can bring not the slightest immediate gain but only an increased 'joie de vivre'."[4] While Köhler is not a behaviorist, yet in his description of purely animal behavior he is forced to use a term "joie de vivre" which has no meaning for one who has not had the immediate experience of pleasure in play. Even more pertinently one may ask what right as an out-and-out behaviorist has Watson to assume that the "men-

[3] *Behaviorism*, W. W. Norton and Company, New York, 1925.

[4] *The Mentality of Apes*, English trans., E. Winter, Harcourt Brace and Company, New York, 1925.

tal state" of rage has anything to do with the howls of protest from a baby when he is forcibly restrained. Clearly, he goes back to the "mental state" in his own mind when subjected to the same treatment.

The prestige which the behaviorist's point of view has acquired in popular thinking has been tremendously augmented by the work of the physiologists in two distinct fields —the study of the so-called "conditioned reflexes" initiated by the great Russian physiologist Ivan Petrovitch Pavlov and the still more recent developments in scientific knowledge of the effects of endocrine secretions upon not only the physical but the mental traits of human individuals.

As a physiologist, initially interested in the study of the digestive process, Pavlov tells us that he "came upon facts of a psychical character, facts which could not be rationally neglected as they participated constantly and prominently in the normal mechanism of the physiological processes."[5] Pavlov's aim was to study these "psychical" factors from the strictly physiological point of view, treating them as elements in the complex problem of the means by which the physico-chemical equilibrium of the life process is maintained. Pavlov did not commit himself to a definition of the term "psychical" as opposed to "physiological" or "physical". He explains the distinction which he makes in his own mind by citing the action of the salivary glands, "organs having apparently a very insignificant physiological role." Food placed in the mouth of an animal immediately stimulates the action of these glands, whose secretion is necessary for the initial step in the digestive process. But it is a matter of observation that the mere sight or scent of food to a dog produces the same reaction. Evidence of any sort leading to the expectation of food stimulates the salivary secretion. How are we to explain this obvious connection between the sense stimulus and the secretory response? Is it necessary to enter

[5] *Lectures on Conditioned Reflexes,* I. P. Pavlov, English trans., G. V. Anvep, Oxford Press, 1927.

into the inner mental state of the animal and to fancy his feelings and wishes as based on our own? Pavlov's answer as an investigator is an unqualified *no*. As he points out, such a reference norm, i.e., our own subjective feelings, is too variable a criterion to serve as any basis for objective truth. Therefore the "first and most important task is to abandon entirely the natural inclination to impose our own subjective condition upon the mechanism of the reaction of the experimental animal and to concentrate our whole attention upon the investigation of the correlation between the external phenomena and the reaction of the organism which in our case is the salivary secretion."[6]

This statement from a truly great scientific mind sets out in sharp relief the limitations of the behavioristic approach in either animal or human psychology. It starts with the physically observable stimulus and ends at the physically observable response. The intermediate steps occurring in the nervous system and brain are to be traced by the strictly scientific method of controlled variables without reference to any conscious process that may or may not accompany these nerve reactions. These steps are described by the term "psychical" as opposed to physical processes on the one hand and conscious mental processes on the other. Pavlov's use of the term corresponds very closely to the sense in which we have used it earlier, namely, that property of living matter by which its behavior is conditioned by future ends as well as by past events. Pavlov states that the field covers an "unlimited territory for successful research in an immense part of the physiology of the nervous system which establishes the relation not only between the individual parts of the organism but between the organism and the surrounding world."[7]

Pavlov's great contribution to the scientific conception of animal behavior was the conditioned reflex, a term which in a great deal of popular thinking seems to put an end to

[6] Ibid.
[7] Ibid.

all ideas of the mind as an effective agent in the control of human conduct. A careful reading of his first lecture delivered in 1903 will confirm the statement that this is far from the truth. To illustrate the difference between the terms conditioned reflex and unconditioned reflex Pavlov cites the secretion of saliva in connection with the presentation of food. The unconditioned reflex is called forth when the food is brought into direct contact with the organism, i.e., when food is placed in the mouth. The stimulation of the salivary glands is, barring abnormal conditions, as certain as the secretion of gastric juice when food is taken into the stomach. When the same result is brought forth simply by the sight or smell of food, the reaction is a conditioned reflex, because numerous factors intervene between the sensory stimulus and the secretory response. For example, if the experimenter simply exhibits the food a number of times without giving it, the response becomes successively weaker with each of these false alarms. It can be restored simply by once making good on the expectation. Pavlov states: "The main characteristic of the psychical experiment is the inconstancy of its results and its apparent capriciousness. The results of a psychical experiment, however, recur with more or less constancy, otherwise we could not speak of it as a scientific experiment."

Pavlov's experimental technique was novel and interesting. The objective criterion of the response in the canine subject was the secretion of saliva. The quantitative determination is made by measuring the rate of salivary flow. The dog is first subjected to a minor operation that consists in the transplanting of the opening of the salivary duct from its natural place in the mucous membrane of the mouth to the outer skin. The saliva thus flows to the outside of the cheek and the rate of flow is measured by an ingenious manometric arrangement with an electric recorder. The experimental animal is placed in a separate chamber from the experimenter, and so far as possible completely isolated from all external stimuli save those which are the immediate object of study. Ideally the experimental situation is thereby reduced to the application of a single stimulus and an objective measurement of the response. The sight of food in the case of a particular subject will be followed in a matter of five seconds by a given rate of flow of saliva. The sensory stimulus arrives at the brain through the organs of sight, and results in a certain activity of the salivary glands. In the next step the sight of food is accompanied by the beating of a metronome. After a few trials, the beating of the metronome without the sight of food elicits the salivary response. The same response in the two cases is elicited by signals, one of which arrives at the central organ by way of the visual, the other by the auditory channel. The connection between the signal and the response is set up in both cases in the brain. This connection is the conditioned reflex and is established as a result of the animal's individual experience. Apart from this experience, neither the sight of food itself nor the sound of the metronome has any observable connection in the nervous system of the animal with the nerves that control the action of the salivary glands.

The unconditioned reflex, the flow of saliva when food is in the mouth, is assumed to occur in any dog and is referred to as a "specific reflex." The reflex of the other type just described is acquired by experience, and as Pavlov's work showed, has its physical basis either in the brain or in the higher nerve center. His work led to the conclusion that these conditioned reflexes proceed according to laws as rigid as those that govern any other physiological process, and that by the proper technique they can be studied and the laws of their behavior (laws in the sense of the uniformity of their appearances) established without any reference to internal conscious processes.

It is highly essential for our purpose, in view of the widespread and very profound effect which Pavlov's work has had both on psychologists and on popular thinking, to make clear his own view of the bearing of this work on human psychology. This is very definitely set forth in his lecture delivered before the Lesgaft Scientific Institute of Petrograd in 1923. This lecture is entitled, "The Latest Successes of the Objective Study of the Highest Nervous Activity."[8] At the outset he poses the question, "Why has physiology failed to master the secrets of the animal organism with reference to the highest section of the nervous system, the brain?" His answer is that "the role of physiology in this domain was contested by psychology—a branch of philosophy which does not even belong to the group of natural sciences. Certainly psychology, in so far as it concerns the subjective state of man has a natural right to existence; for our subjective world is the first reality with which we are confronted. But though the right of existence of human psychology be granted, there is no reason why we should not question the necessity of an animal psychology. What means have we to enter the inner world of the animal—what basis for speaking of what an animal feels. The word 'zoo-psychology' is, it seems to me, a misnomer."

This is a clear-cut statement as to the position of the behavioristic method in relation to the problems of human psychology. Whether the object of behavioristic study be Pavlov's dogs or the babies in Watson's researches, the facts gained relate only to the analysis and synthesis effected by the brain and nervous system of the animal, canine or human. That the laws by which this analysis and synthesis are effected should be definite is a necessary condition for the maintenance of the organism as a going concern. That there is no sort of *mechanical* necessity involved in their operation is fully evidenced by the fact of individual differences that biological and psychological experiments always reveal to the embarrassment of the thorough-going mechanist.

[8] *Lectures on Conditioned Reflexes*, I. P. Pavlov, English trans., W. H. Gantt, Martin Lawrence, London, 1929.

It is obvious enough that the facts and laws of conditioned response brought out by animal experimentation and by work of similar import on young children should exert a powerful influence on psychological thought and methods. That these findings should lead to broad generalizations that are far beyond their strictly scientific implications is a fact that is much more apt to occur in a field like psychology than in the mathematical sciences—where theories can be checked by crucial experiments, the results of which are not subject to equivocal interpretation. The extreme behavioristic position is to the effect that all human conduct flows from the operation of conditioned reflexes built up on a few primitive emotions (Watson limits these to fear, rage, and love) by conditioning or training; that thought consists in implicit movements of the speech organs, and that the emotions consist largely in implicit behavior of the viscera. Such a philosophy, for it must be called a philosophy since it involves an interpretation of facts quite beyond the established facts themselves, relegates the idea of the mind as a creative factor either in individual conduct or in racial evolution to the limbo of unscientific superstitions. For mechanistic determinism it substitutes not psychological but physiological determinism and leaves the individual a helpless and therefore an irresponsible victim of his innate impulses, and the conditioning factors which from his infancy impose themselves upon him from without.

This is the tenor of a philosophy, based on an observational study of the conditioned responses of the nervous system of dogs and the behavior of human babies, which a few decades ago was hailed with widespread popular approval as the cold unassailable facts of a psychology that had finally freed itself from the speculations of metaphysics. Behaviorism commands our respect, even if not our acceptance, both for its antiquity and for its practical results. One may find its classical prototype in the atomism of Democritus and Lucretius, and in more modern guise it appears in the philosophy of Comte and the positivists and the psychology of James Mill. The "tough-minded" philosopher has always denied reality to everything which does not enter the mind through the gateway of the senses. What cannot be objectively perceived does not exist. All that can be observed in animal and human behavior is the external stimulus and the response of the organism, the two being connected by a chain of conditioned reflexes that can be explained by physical, psychical, or whatever changes that can occur in the nervous system without reference to conscious processes. Therefore, reasons our behaviorist philosopher, mental processes can have no influence on human conduct.

The practical applications of the conditioned reflex are found in any kind of an educational process. Every animal trainer uses exactly the same technique that Pavlov used or that the farmer's wife uses when she beats on the side of the feed-pan to call her hens. Institutional religions are perpetuated by "conditioning" the minds of the young. Political parties maintain in no small degree their hold on the popular mind by associating a given set of political shibboleths with the innate impulse of fear and another set with the hope of reward or pleasure. Modern advertising utilizes the behavioristic technique to the nth degree. Good advertising consists in associating the response to some pleasurable sensation with the suggestion of the article that is advertised. Propaganda is the application of the method to the control of the behavior of an entire population.

Thus behaviorism, an old, old, idea by a brand new name, has achieved practical triumphs that commend it most highly to the practical spirit of our generation. But what of its claims to being an adequate account of the human mind? Does it present a self-consistent picture of the conscious personal self? Descartes, in his search for an absolute certainty upon which to build a structure of thought that would encompass all reality, set up his famous dictum "I *think,* therefore I *am.*" Behaviorism, on the other hand, starting with sensory stimuli and ending with conditioned responses, entirely short circuits the *I* and the *thinking*. Behaviorism, starting with a pair of robot-fertilized germ cells and subjecting one to that particular set of stimuli to which this particular bit of protoplasm I call myself has been subjected, and the other to your particular train of stimuli, would arrive at the end with a pair of adult robots which behavioristically would be *I* and *you*. The robots would behave exactly as I and you behave, and that would be all there is to the pair of us.

Pavlov's work with dogs showed conclusively that the operation of any particular conditioned reflex depends not only upon the present stimulus but upon past experience involving that reflex. The reflex flow of saliva upon the sight of food is extinguished in an animal whose past experience has been that the presentation of food to sight is *not* followed by its delivery to the mouth. The reflex is inhibited. This certainly implies that there is a thread of continuity between the past experience and the present situation. We may, if we like, assume that the inhibition is the result of some subtle chemical change that takes place somewhere along the nerve track between the sensory and motor nerves. Making this assumption, we are met with the difficulty that this chemical change was brought about by a purely nonphysical influence, the breaking of the usual sequence between the sight and the delivery of the food. The assumption of a chemical change thus effected violates the mechanistic principle that physical results can follow only physical causes. The other horn of the dilemma is to assume a psychical change in the nervous mechanism, a change in which both past and future have a determining influence in the present event—a situation exactly that which at the conscious level we call choice. In inhibition either the reflex arc is broken as a result of a physical change produced by a nonphysical cause, or a power of choice must be somewhere inherent in the nature of nerve or brain tissue. The psychological determinism implicit in the radical behavioristic position is thus seen to rest on very shaky logical foundations.

It would seem that the acceptance of extreme behaviorism either precludes the possibility of evolution in man at the conscious level, or else it admits the evolutionary urge, whatever that may mean, as an effective stimulus of human behavior. Pavlov adopted the view that both unconditioned and conditioned reflexes are a necessary part of the process by which a complex organism adapts itself to a complex environment.

The sense organs analyze the elements of the environment. The brain and the higher nerve centers, through the direct and conditioned reflexes, control the response of the organism in such a way that the proper adjustments are made to insure survival. A moment's consideration on the introspective side will convince us that a very large part of our own behavior is governed in this way by reflex responses that never enter the field of consciousness. The eyelid closes to protect the eye from a flying cinder in much less time than it takes to think about it. We reflexively dodge an impending blow, or catch ourselves when about to fall. In the acquirement of any skill requiring coordination of muscular movements we set up a series of reflex arcs from which consciousness is excluded. These are all activities that have to do with our behavior as animal organisms. They are a part of the process of adaptation. If, as Pavlov contends, the study of conditioned reflexes in animals belongs properly within the scope of physiology, then that part of human behavior which is governed by the same sort of processes properly comes under the head of human physiology rather than psychology. That is to say, nothing is gained in the way of scientific description by invoking conscious experience in explanation of phenomena that can be adequately described in physiological terms.

But does the behavioristic hypothesis cover the whole field of the operation of what we shall insist upon calling the human mind? Can the behaviorist in terms of his own premises account for his own behavior as a searcher after truth? The answer is, I think, an unqualified negative. Granted that "behavioristic behavior", that the human animal exhibits in common with other animals, has survival value, is this the whole story as to why we behave like *human* beings? Biologically, the outstanding difference between the human species and the rest of the animal world lies in this, that *human* intelligence exhibits itself most markedly in the active modification of the environment to the demands of the human organism, whereas *animal* intelligence shows itself in the more passive adaptation of the organism to the necessities imposed by the environment. This is evidenced by the fact that man is the only species that is able to survive under any and all of the climatic conditions that exist upon the globe.

This capacity for what one may call creative adaptation goes with the more highly developed brain of genus *homo*. Human evolution proceeds in the direction of an ever increasing power of creative adaptation. The purely biological and anatomical differences between the Neanderthal man and modern civilized man are insignificant. The difference that is really significant, that represents the result of hundreds of thousands of years of human evolution, is in the increased mastery that modern man has achieved over external nature. The domestication of animals, the cultivation of the earth, the discovery of fire, the invention of primitive mechanical devices, the utilization of the power of steam and electricity—all testify to a creative capacity inherent in the total human organism that belongs in an entirely different category from the conditioned responses to which behaviorism would ascribe all human activity. The creative faculty does not arise as a result of the action of the external world upon the human organism, but rather from an inner urge of that element in man's nature which is the essence of his "human-ness".

To the modifications, whatever they may be, in the cerebral synapses which are the seat of conditioned reflexes, individual man adds the experience stored in conscious memory. To the immediate response called forth by environmental stimuli, he adds the power of sustained activity directed to the accomplishment of far distant future ends. In addition to the drives of sex and hunger he may, and does, in all that is *human* in the highest sense, respond to ideas of values which transcend the instinctive urge for mere survival. Behaviorism may explain why we behave as animals. It leaves out of the picture entirely why we behave as human beings.

At the opposite pole from the behavioristic concept of the human mind is that of the psychoanalytic school of psychology introduced by Freud, Adler and Jung. The influence of the psychoanalytic movement has been profound and far reaching, not only in psychology but in literature and art as well as in popular thought. The *complex, fixation, dreams, the ego, transference, the super-ego, symbolism, libido* have all found their way into the conversation of the sophisticated and the language of the modern novel. Surrealism in art and the "stream of consciousness" in fiction purport to have their roots in the depths of the "unconscious", on which psychoanalysis lays so much stress. Behaviorism, the child begotten in psychological thought of four hundred years of objective physical science, reduces mental experiences to epiphenomena that accompany but do not control physical processes in the brain and nervous system. The fundamental assumption of psychoanalysis is that the *psyche* (to use the term of the psychoanalysts) has a real existence, in and of itself, that is not to be explained or expressed in terms of physico-chemical reactions in the nervous tissue of the organism. Its relation to the brain is not that of effect to cause, but rather it is assumed that psychical activity and cerebral activity have a causal connection which operates both ways. Consciousness is the point of fusion between the inner and the outer reality. Jung puts it thus: "Although our mind cannot grasp its own form of existence, owing to the lack of an

Archimedean point outside, it nevertheless exists. Psyche is existent, it is even existence itself."[9]

But psychoanalysis does not limit the individual psyche to the conscious mind alone, or even to that which can voluntarily be brought to the level of consciousness. Just as the huge bulk of the iceberg that towers above the surface of the ocean is only a small part of that which is concealed below, so the conscious mind is but a portion of the psychical unity that finds expression in the personality of the individual. This submerged portion, the *unconscious,* is not quiescent and inert. Quite on the contrary, it plays an active role in the emotional and volitional life of the individual. In it are enfolded not only the permanent living records of all the past experiences of the individual himself, but also the drives and urges of past centuries and millenniums that come to him through his heredity· From it there intrude into conscious life all sorts of irrational and involuntary impulses that find expression in many cases in behavior which the individual cannot account for to himself. According to the analytical view the unconscious throws its shadows into the conscious in the symbolism of dreams. It betrays itself as a disturbing factor in such every day occurrences as slips of the tongue, mistakes in reading or writing, or in the failure to remember a familiar name. In extreme cases it becomes the seat of those disorders in the nervous and mental life characterized as neuroses. All of these activities of the unconscious play no part upon the stage of consciousness of the normally functioning mind. They are, so to speak, unseen prompters behind the scenes.

Two questions occur to the matter-of-fact mind of the scientist. "What sort of an existence can possibly be ascribed to something that must exist in the mind and yet in its very nature is concealed from conscious mental processes? What possible experimental data can be adduced for be-

[9] C. G. Jung, *Modern Man in Search of a Soul,* Harcourt Brace, New York, 1933.

lieving that it exists at all?" The psychoanalyst answers by posing a question in kind. "What possible experimental data can you adduce for believing in the existence of matter, when all you have is a body of sense experiences that are not matter at all? You as a physicist postulate the independent existence of an unknown something which you call *matter* and to which you ascribe certain properties by which you can fashion into a coherent whole the results of physical experiments. As a psychologist I postulate the existence of an unknown something which I call the *unconscious* by which I can fit psychological facts into a conceptual unity." Just what are these empirical facts upon which the psychoanalyst bases his belief in the existence of the "unconscious" as a potent factor in human personality?

Much of the knowledge that medical science has of the functional interrelations of the organs of the body has come from the study of the effects of disease. The mal-functioning of the sick body throws light on the normal functioning of the healthy body. Similarly, psychoanalysis had its origin not in psychology but in psychiatry. Sigmund Freud, the founder of the psychoanalytic school, was at the outset a physician, specializing in diseases of the nervous system. His interests centered largely in those cases in which no organic disorders can be discovered and yet in which a wide variety of pathological symptoms appear, cases which are the bane of the existence of the medical practitioner, which he classes under the general head of *hysteria* and tries to pass on to some colleague whom he doesn't like. Medical science had long recognized that these cases are to be traced to psychical rather than to physiological causes, and that, although there are no ascertainable organic lesions to account for them, yet the symptoms are real in the sense that they are beyond the conscious control of the patient. In short, the *neurotic* is ill with an illness that cannot be traced either to his body or to his conscious mind. The problem of diagnosis and cure is within the province of psychiatry rather than medicine. But how is the psychiatrist to penetrate this region of human personality that is to be reached neither by way of the physical body nor the conscious mind? It is to the genius and profound insight of Sigmund Freud that the credit is to be ascribed for the discovery of the method by which the dynamic qualities of the unconscious can be observed, the relation of its elements studied, as well as the tremendous influence it exerts on the mental and physical health of both the normal subject and the pathologically neurotic. As so often happens to the discoverer of a new truth, Freud came in for his full share of opprobrium and censure, not only from other specialists in his field, but from the modern counterparts of that type of so-called religious minds that would have burned Galileo at the stake and that anathematized Darwin and his doctrine of evolution.

It must be admitted that the first effect of the Freudian view of personality was apparently to undermine the very foundation of Christian faith, belief in the existence of the "human soul," the image in man of his Creator. The "psyche" of psychoanalysis is something profoundly different from the "soul" of Christian theology. It is a living, growing thing whose roots go down deep into the primal animal instincts of man. Medieval asceticism and modern Puritanism have conditioned a great deal of religious thinking to the point at which we feel "the spirit" and "the flesh" as continuously at war with each other. The prayer sometimes offered in the rite of infant baptism that "all carnal desires may die in this child" fails to recognize the effect which the universal answer to this prayer would have upon the church-going population of a generation hence. In this petition there is a vestige of that early reaction of the Stoic element injected into early Christian teaching against the sensuality of a decadent Roman civilization. We recognize further that what we are really asking for in behalf of the child is an integrated personality, in which the image of God will not be obliterated by the rank growth of the instinctive drives that are necessary for the perpetuation of the species.

In evaluating Freud's contribution to the knowledge of human personality, it is necessary to distinguish between psychoanalysis as a method and as psychological theory. As already intimated, its origin was in Freud's attempt to discover the causes of neuroses. Starting with the assumption that the source of the neurotic's illness is in the unconscious, hypnosis and hypnotic suggestion were tried as means of arriving at the origin of the difficulty. It had been used by J. M. Charcot, Morton Prince, Boris Sidis, and others with measurable, though not outstanding, success. Freud abandoned the method in favor of that which has since become characteristic of the analytical approach, namely the method of "free association". The patient is asked to put himself in as quiescent a state as possible, and, freeing himself from all conscious control, to say whatever occurs to him to say, regardless of its logic, relevancy or politeness. The analyst's attitude is that of a completely impersonal recipient of these disclosures, the more passive his attitude the better, since anything in the nature of an active reaction on the part of the doctor calls into play the conscious factors in the patient, which have to be eliminated if the unconscious layers are to be reached. The psychological technique might be compared to that of the oculist when he paralyzes the accommodation mechanism of the eye in order to determine the refraction of the lens free from muscular control. Here we see also something of the same psychological situation as exists in the confessional of the Catholic Church, but without the moral and religious implications of the latter. Under these conditions, thoughts, feelings, wishes and memories that are not part of the patient's conscious experience come to the surface and find expression in words, from which the psychiatrist may deduce the unconscious material that is the source of the neurosis.

Applying this technique to his patients, Freud found

that in every case of neurotic disturbance in which the procedure was successful, there existed a conflict or state of tension between the "repressed" unconscious elements and the dominant moral tendencies of the patient's conscious life. The content of the unconscious further reveals itself in the patient's dreams, not in overt form but in symbols and allusions that require interpretation. Freud maintained that dreams properly interpreted turn out to be wish fulfilments. In many cases the wish is conscious and the interpretation is relatively easy. But more often the wish is not admitted by the conscious self and the symbolism and associations called up by the dream are the expression of unconscious tendencies that are not consonant with the conscious subject's moral standards, and which consciously he rejects. The discovery of these unconscious wishes reveals the conflict responsible for the neurosis. The analysis then consists in the interpretation by the analyst, with the patient's aid, of the material brought to consciousness by the free association method and the dreams. The therapeutic effect follows from the conscious recognition by the patient of the conflict between the conscious and unconscious elements and the integration of the personality that can be effected in the light of this recognition. In short, psychoanalysis is a means by which the neurotic individual can carry out the Delphic injunction "Know Thyself."

This is a brief and nontechnical account of the essential features of the psychoanalytic method in psychiatry as it appears to a layman from a study of Freud's own voluminous writings. The psychoanalyst maintains that the mental cures resulting from the application of the method constitute a scientific basis for the assumption on which it is based—the existence of the unconscious as a dynamic element of human personality. Today the method is recognized by a large body of psychiatrists as an effective means of psychotherapy. The facts of suggestion and hypnosis, as well as one's own self-analysis of the multitude of irrational impulsions and urges for which one can find no conscious motivation, has led to a very general acceptance of the existence of the unconscious in the Freudian sense.

From his findings by the use of the psychoanalytic method, Freud was led to a general theory of the structure and organization of the psyche. This called forth on the one hand a perfect storm of criticism, and on the other complete and enthusiastic acceptance. The first resulted from the fact that the Freudian psychology centers largely in the sexual instincts. Why this particular era in which we live should be so completely irrational one way or the other on this specific biological fact will form an interesting chapter in the social history of our day when it comes to be written with the clear perspective of time. Whatever the explanation may be, it is a matter of record that the emphasis which Freud placed on the sexual, not only in the origin of pathological states, but in the development of the normal personality, was enough to damn his theories completely in the minds of those for whom this side of man's nature is an invention of the devil. It is quite explicable that, dealing as Freud did with those types of mental illness that psychiatrists have long recognized as arising largely either from sexual abnormalities or sexual maladjustments, he should with the one-sidedness of genius overemphasize the role played by this powerful force in making or marring the individual personality. But it would seem that this overemphasis is not misplaced when we consider that the family is the unit of our social order, and that its solidarity rests very largely upon the psychological relations of the parents to each other and to their offspring, and that, further, these psychological relations are rooted deep in the fact that the mind as well as the body of the child is bisexual in its origin.

The psychical equipment of the child at birth, according to Freud's view, comprises impersonal elements of the psyche which he calls the Id. The Id consists of the innate urges and inherited tendencies, and is the source of the instinctive psychical energy of the individual. It is dominated by the pleasure principle and is amoral and illogical. In short, it is the native urge to pleasurable activity. Its strongest drive is sexual. Incidentally it may be said that much of the opposition to Freud's views on moral grounds arises from the very wide sense in which he uses his term "sex". It appears that his theories would have encountered much less violent opposition had he found some word that is free from the usual specific connotations of the term "sexual." His own definition states that "sexuality is to be regarded as a comprehensive bodily function having pleasure as its goal, and includes all those affectionate impulses to which usage applies the extremely ambiguous term 'love' ".

The Ego is the organization of mental life from the primal content of the Id resulting from contact of the individual with the outer world. It includes both conscious and unconscious elements, and represents what we call reason and sanity. In the normal person it regulates the drives that originate in the Id. It has the power to accept or *repress* the impulses arising in the Id. It represents that power of the conscious self by which the individual adapts himself to his physical and social environment.

The Super-ego is an outgrowth and modification of the Ego, and results, according to the psychoanalysts, from the early psychological identification of the child with his parents. It has its origin in the commands and prohibitions of parental control and becomes a dynamic element in the censorship which it exercises over the Ego. It is a permanent expression not only of parental training but of the intimate psychical relation between the parents and the child. It is the critical faculty that the mind exercises on its own activities, and corresponds to what is ordinarily meant by the word "conscience." As conceived in the Freudian view it is not a God-given power of the individual soul but rather a normal development that begins with the egoistic tendencies of the child as they are affected by parental influence and later by the opinions and judgments of others. In normal psychical life the Id has been likened to the motor that supplies the power, the Ego to the driver at the controls who recognizes the traffic signals and the dangers of the road, while the Super-ego plays the role of a pleasant companion with a road map who suggests the necessary turnings. An overdeveloped Super-ego is tyrannical and becomes a troublesome back seat driver whose excessive criticism may result in a smashup which the psychiatrist calls a neurosis.

We cannot go into the elaborate detail in which Freud develops his theory of the organization and structure of the mind. Much of it has meaning only for those whose experiences have made them familiar with the distorted mental patterns that appear in the mentally and nervously sick. Much of it is illuminating to the normal mind of even a slightly introspective turn in explaining those irrational elements in thought and impulse of which we are all more or less unpleasantly aware. Its absorbing interest in popular thinking is evidenced by the remarkable degree to which it has influenced modern fiction and drama. We are interested, however, in one or two points that are pertinent to the new world-view that science opens to the modern mind.

First we note that the psyche as conceived by psychoanalysis is organic in the sense that it follows a fixed pattern of growth and development and that its elements are functionally related to each other, and to the psychical elements of its environment. In its growth it follows the general biological and evolutionary pattern from the relatively simple and uncoordinated to the differentiated and functionally coordinated. The simple urge to pleasurable activity of the Id has its counterpart in the irritability of the protoplasm of the living cell. The development of the elemental psyche of the infant through its "hormic" (to use McDougal's, rather than Freud's term) responses to parental care and affection, to the adult personality, responsive to and creative in a highly complex social environment, is quite analogous to the marvelous physiological development that marks the progress from the fertilized ovum to the fully developed adult. Just as the body of the child bears the imprint of its heredity from the parents, so the psyche of the child bears hereditary characters and also characters that are psychically transmitted from both parents during the preadolescent period. Just as permanent injury in the physical life of an individual may result from adverse conditions during infancy, so lasting consequences to his psychical life may result from adverse psychical elements in preadolescence.

Further we note that the dynamic qualities of the psyche make it potentially creative. The Ego, while subject on the one hand to the impulsions of the Id, and on the other hand to the censorship of the Super-ego, has nevertheless a limited power of choice, within which it may move toward its own self-created ends. Therein we see it as an expression of the Creator spirit in which the past and the future are fused in the consciousness and activities of the present moment.

Finally we can see, I think, in the psychoanalytic concept of the human psyche some faint glimmering of the solution of the problem of the "one and the many". From the standpoint of conscious experience each of us thinks of himself as a complete unit separate and distinct from all other units of consciousness. *I* am *I*, independently of all other conscious existences. Yet, if we accept the existence of the unconscious, the *I* of self-recognition is only one aspect of the total reality that constitutes my personality. Looking at the matter along the time axis, that total reality includes the accumulations of all my past individual experiences, plus the immediately transmitted elements of the Super-ego that came from my parents before consciousness of self arose. To that must be added that psychical inheritance from the past, stretching back in an unbroken chain of human ancestry, and if we accept evolution, to the very origin of life itself.

Subjectively, the conscious self is the particle aspect,

discrete, separate, individual. Objectively, the psyche is the wave aspect—not a separate existence but simply a localization in time and space of a universal psychical being. Who can say of any particular moment in his existence, "Before that moment I was not I," or "at such and such a time I came into being." One looks at one's "family tree" and realizes that the generations of one's forebears constitute a continuous unbroken line of germ plasm through which not only the physical but the psychical life from an immemorial past flows into the present of one's own existence. But we must further consider the fact that while genealogy is traced only through the male parent, yet one's complete heredity comes from two parents, four grandparents, eight great-grandparents, and so on, in ascending powers of two. It is a matter of easy calculation to show that, barring intermarriage, the total number of one's ancestors who lived in the tenth century would be some eight billions of grandparents, each one of whom contributed something in the matter of inheritance to his or her grandchild of the thirtieth order in the present generation. Consciously, the *I* which is *I* is "one". Genetically it is "many". As Oliver Wendell Holmes has put it, "We are omnibuses in which ride the ghosts of our ancestors."

There is also a very real sense in which, in the present, the psyche reaches beyond the individual unity of the conscious self. "I am a part of all I have met" may with equal truth be stated the other way round, "All I have met has be come a part of me." If we take the trouble to consider the matter at all, we are all aware how powerfully childhood experiences may color the whole emotional background of mature life. In his comprehensive study *Varieties of Religious Experience,* William James reaches the conclusion that the phenomenon of sudden religious conversion is seldom if ever encountered in persons who have not in childhood been subjected to the influences of evangelistic teachings. The individual may have long since abandoned these early ideas, but they are still a part of his unconscious, and may under conditions of strong emotional stress result in those sudden transformations of life purpose and world-view which seem miraculous rebirths of the personality. On the other hand, reading Schopenhauer, one wonders why, on his fundamental postulate of "The World as Will and Idea," he should arrive at a completely pessimistic world-view. The wonder is resolved when we learn of the bitter relationship between Schopenhauer and his mother, and find therein an unconscious emotional motivation that did not have its origin in the rational processes of his thought.

Even more do we see this operation of the extra-personal elements of the psyche in those vast surges of mass emotion that sweep over a whole nation, waves of feeling that carry the conscious mind far from its moorings, bearing the educated and the ignorant alike into ecstasies of devotion to a leader or a cause that, viewed in the cold light of reason, is repellent to the highest human ideals. We in America, with our tradition of democracy and political freedom, were filled with amazement that German friends whom we knew to be men of rational temper should have joined with the ignorant masses in their fanatical zeal and devotion to "der Fuehrer". Explanation can only be found when we consider how deep in the unconscious of the Teutonic mind are those myths and legends of the pagan gods and heroes, the prototypes of the "superman" of Nietzsche's philosophy of the will to power.

The first World War, with its ruthless savagery and ultimate humiliation of the German people, left a very thin crust of rational repression over the volcanic power of the unconscious mind of the nation. The old Teutonic gods still lived in the German psyche, and with them the dream of a savior, the leader, the superman of Nietzschean philosophy and Wagnerian drama. It is no miracle that this unconscious heritage of a whole people should find expression in the frenzied oratory of an Adolf Hitler. *Mein Kampf* flowed from Hitler's pen, but in a very real sense it surged up from the Id of some sixty millions of Germans.

That this seems strange to us with what we call our "ideals of freedom", arises from the fact that in our unconscious lies an equally intense and equally nonrational *individualism* that we have rationalized under the euphonies of "democracy, liberty and equality." In our psychical heritage, whether our ancestors happened to have landed on Plymouth Rock or at Ellis Island, is the unconscious drive to freedom from restraint and to individual initiative. Love of freedom is ours by a process of natural selection, accentuated by three centuries of economic growth in which this drive has found full expression and ample reward in subduing the wilderness and in building a great industrial civilization. Faced with a new economic situation as we are today, in which the distribution rather than the production of material wealth is a paramount problem of our national life, we find ourselves confused and helpless in making the psychological adjustment to a situation that calls for the coordination of individual effort in social objectives. The unconscious will to power cloaks itself in the "rugged individualism" that insists upon the maintenance of the economic status quo. No less does it hide in the unconscious motivation of ambition that rides on the tide of social reform to political power and preferment. Thus we have only to recognize the existence of the unconscious as a potent factor in individual psychology to realize the tremendous part which it plays in the great mass movements of human history.

C. G. Jung has seen in these facts of social behavior the basis for belief in the existence of a "collective unconscious". He says, "It is to my mind a fatal mistake to consider the human psyche as a merely personal affair and to explain it exclusively from a personal point of view."[10] Freud stoutly maintained the ascendency of sexual instinct as the chief psychic driving power and explained group psychology in

[10] Ibid.

terms of individual psychology. Jung substituted for the sexual the sum total of all the psychic drives, and extended the individual unconscious to include a still deeper layer common to the whole race. In this assumption we find explanation of those vast psychic tides in human affairs such as the rapid spread of Christianity during the first centuries of the Christian era, the Crusades, the Renaissance and the Reformation. But more specifically, Jung finds in the unconscious material brought to the surface in the analytic interpretations of the dreams of his neurotic patients symbolisms of specific types that recur repeatedly in the rituals and practices of cults and religions of which the patients themselves have no conscious knowledge. Finally, the appearance in many different forms of essentially the same ideas in the teachings of religions of widely separated origins points to a common psychical element, out of which these ideas arise and to which they appeal. It is as if the individual unconscious springs from the racial unconscious just as shoots appear above ground from a rhizome buried beneath the surface. Jung finds in this no reason for deprecating the importance of religion as a factor in human psychology, but rather reason for the recognition of the religious drive, stemming as it does from the depth of man's being, as a psychic element of supreme significance in the evolution of the human spirit. Magic, folklore, mythologies and religions, arising under the most diverse conditions among primitive peoples in widely different parts of the world, have in their psychological contents so much in common that Jung maintains they must come from a common source, the racial unconscious, the matrix of the individual unconscious and the substratum from which the Ego develops the unity of conscious life.

But Jung goes still further and finds the origin of what he calls the "visionary modes of artistic creation" in this same "hinterland" of the mind. Dante's *Inferno,* Goethe's *Faust,* Wagner's *Nibelungenring,* and the poetry of William Blake are cited as examples of literature of this type. All of these, so he maintains, are not begotten of the artist's personal experience, but come from the primordial soul of man and bring a message to the conscious mind of the living generation in the imagery of a great work of art.

Jung's conception of the collective unconscious is of course quite beyond the possibility of proof, but with a wealth of illustrative material drawn from anthropology, philology and literature he establishes good grounds for belief in the psychical unity of mankind.

Much has been written by way of explanation in psychological terms of the creativeness of genius. Is it not more than possible that the greatness of a work of art in the sense of the universality of its appeal lies in this, that in the creative artist the partition separating the individual consciousness from the psychical life of the race is permeable as are the walls of a living cell to the life-carrying fluid of its environment, so that the artist simply brings to expression in the sensuous forms of poetry, painting, or music that which is already in the individual unconscious of all? May it not be that the very quality of greatness, universality of appeal, lies in the fact that the unconscious becomes a living experience for the creative artist himself and in turn is re-created in the work of art that induces the same living experience in others? The artist sees and feels back of nature and back of his own consciousness a world of psychical reality that can only be communicated through the medium of his art. In the very fact that this same reality exists in the collective unconscious, and hence potentially in the conscious experience of other men, and is brought to the level of emotional awareness by the work of art—in this lies the creativeness of the artist. The greatness of a great poem or a great painting is not only something achieved in the skill of its fabrication, but lies also in the fact that out of the chaos of the unconscious has been created a sensuous form which can evoke in the sensitive soul that same awareness of "oneness with the whole" which inspired it.

In his essay on "Psychology and Literature",[11] Jung develops this idea in terms of his Analytical Psychology. He says: "It makes no difference whether the poet knows that his work is begotten, grows and matures with him, or whether he supposes that by taking thought he produces it out of the void. His opinion of the matter does not change the fact that his own work outgrows him as a child its mother. The creative process has feminine quality and the creative work arises from unconscious depth—we might say—from the realm of the mothers. Whenever the creative force predominates, human life is ruled by the unconscious as against the active will—'it is not Goethe who creates *Faust* but Faust who creates Goethe.' " Further, speaking of the redemptive function of the artist, or perhaps better of the work of art, he says, "When conscious life is characterized by one-sidedness and by a false attitude, then they (the primordial images of poetic vision) are activated—one might say, 'instinctively'—and come to light in the dreams of individuals and the visions of artists and seers, thus restoring the psychic equilibrium of the epoch."

The history of art affords numerous instances of this redeeming balancing quality in artistic creation. It is something more than mere coincidence that the revival in art, in painting and architecture was the forerunner of the birth of modern science, and, in religion, of the Reformation. It was as if the sensitive psyche of the artist first became aware of the one-sidedness of the medieval mind in its preoccupation with metaphysical religiosity of scholasticism and in its own language said to the world "Enough of all this. There still is beauty, and beauty is truth."

It is easy to believe that the galaxy of great names, Giotto, Van Eyck, Botticelli, Titian, Leonardo and a host of others that made the fourteenth and fifteenth centuries the golden age in the history of art owed their inspiration to a common urge not fully to be explained by external condi-

[11] Ibid.

tions. Who shall say that the truth in beauty that speaks to the emotions rather than to the intellect was not the spark which kindled anew the quest for rational truth in the order of nature, which had for centuries been neglected by the intellect of the Middle Ages?

If we turn to the modern arts, literature, painting, music and sculpture, we find ourselves lost in bewilderment in our search for the redemptive function that Jung ascribes to the creativeness of artistic genius. Much that lays claim to modernity in all the arts reflects only the conscious sense of futility, frustration and despair that seems to be the heritage of an age gone mad. In much of modern fiction one finds the bitter cynicism engendered in sensitive spirits by the ruthless cruelty of greed and the lust for power. Our writers hold the mirror up to nature and find reflected there only the dark and hateful side of humanity. In their conscious attempts to plumb the depths of the unconscious they bring to the surface only the gross and ugly. Under the guise of *realism* they ignore things that are "lovely and of good report," portraying that which is worst rather than that which is best. For writers of this school only the sordid and the unwholesome are real.

In painting and sculpture so-called "modernism" runs riot in an orgy of isms and cults. Futurism, Cubism, Expressionism, Dadaism, Surrealism appear on the stage in rapid succession, each going to greater and greater extremes of sensationalism and absurdity in their attempts to escape the conventional and the stereotyped. Dimly aware of the drive of the unconscious, in a blind revolt against the half truths of Impressionism, that entirely miss the depths of tragic beauty of a living world, the Modernists have abandoned all notion of art as representative of anything save the untempered agitations of the artist's own spirit. Like literature, a vast deal of modern painting is the voice of protest raised against the spirit of our times, a spirit in which the truth that lies in beauty is crushed beneath the hard, cold weight of a materialistic culture. Truly there is a one-sidedness in the psychology of our generation in the overwhelming emphasis that is placed upon material achievement and the physical mastery of the forces of nature. But for the most part artists of our time have been able to do little more than show the symptoms of our collective neurosis in the primitive, meaningless, absurdities that go under the name of "modernism" in art and literature.

In order to find the really redemptive note in the art of recent times we shall have to go back to the end of the last century. It is in July of 1890. In a cheap little inn at Auvers near Paris, a man of thirty-seven is dying. Nature probably never fashioned a more repellent exterior. Of him as of another it could truly be said "he was despised and rejected of men." Homely to the point of repugnance with bristly red hair and beard, he has protruding brows beneath which a pair of watery blue eyes look out, now with the innocent blankness of a baby, now with the fierce brilliance of the fanatic. One large ear sticks out rudely from the closely cropped head. The other is missing. Dying and in cruel pain, he talks quietly of art to his brother Theo. Always through the years it was in the patient and understanding heart of his brother that Vincent Van Gogh found refuge from the fierce tempests that swept his soul. Now he is saying "Well, my own work, I have risked my life for it and my reason has half foundered.—Do you know what I think of pretty often? That, even if I have not succeeded, all the same what I have worked at will be carried on—not directly, but one isn't alone in believing in things that are true. And what does it matter, personally, then? I feel so strongly that it is with people as it is with corn; if you are not sown in the earth to spring there, what does it matter? You are ground between the millstones to become bread. The difference between happiness and unhappiness! Both are necessary and useful; and death and disappearance, they are so relative, and life the same."[12]

These are not the words of a Christian martyr, but they do sound a new note—that note of sacrificial atonement which first came to the level of human consciousness nineteen centuries earlier in the life and death of the Galilean mystic. They have their roots deep in the unconscious. Years before, Vincent had written, "I am drawn more and more to the conclusion that to love much is the best means of approaching God. I am trying to save my soul. I love these poor miners. Disdaining marble, clay and color, I work in living flesh and blood as did Christ, the greatest of all artists."[13]

The tragedy of Van Gogh's life lay in the fact that blessed, or perhaps from the personal point of view, cursed, with an infinite capacity of love for his fellow men, he elicited nothing but repugnance and scorn from others. At the age of twenty-seven, almost completely unskilled in technique, he turned to painting as a medium for the expression of the love that was in him. In the ten years left to him he labored like the madman, which to all intents and practical purposes he was, toward the mastery of a technique, never finished and always crude, yet one which was peculiarly his own and which places him in the front rank of the painters of all times. His greatness does not lie in the technical perfection, but rather in the fusion which the white heat of his genius or his madness effected between nature and the human spirit.

Within him burned the love of the Christ for his fellow men, and within him too was the poignant sense of the suffering soul of the world, the mute patient endurance of the peasant, the broken mutilated life of the pollarded willows, the livid glow of sunflowers on twisted tortuous stems—all these were the externals of the creative drive of his own suf-

[12] *Dear Theo* (Life of Van Gogh), Irving Stone, Houghton, Mifflin Company, Boston, 1937.

[13] Ibid.

fering spirit, a consuming fire in which the soul of the artist was fused in the soul of things. And out of the unescapable necessity to put into form and color the visions which he both saw and created, grew that individual style that combined the technical mastery of the Impressionists with the vivid almost frenzied expression of his own intense feeling. If we were to attempt to express in rational terms the specific content of the unconscious brought to the surface of consciousness by Van Gogh's painting, I should say it is just this—that the essence of all authentic experience lies in the essential psychical unity of mankind and in an underlying spiritual union between the human psyche and the world of nature. The emphasis that our civilization lays on the importance of individual effort, the insistence on the uniqueness and independent existence of the individual human soul, the atomism of the older scientific world-view—all have conspired to enhance that illusory sense of individual isolation, which on the one hand accentuates the aggressive egoism of a competitive society, and on the other destroys the capacity of modern man for any sort of mystical religious experience. Primitive man feels himself one with his tribe and with nature. Civilized man thinks of himself as separate and distinct from and at war with both man and nature. Through the genius of Vincent Van Gogh, the racial unconscious speaks to the consciousness of an age of riotous individualism of a unity of man with man and of man with nature, a unity that ties the individual to the whole and in spite of all differences binds the soul of each to the common lot of all.

We are apt to think of the unconscious as the seat of those loathsome and hateful elements of human nature, the dark cellars of the mind from which lust and hate and all evil emerge. If we follow Jung's conception of it, we shall picture it also as the source of the inspiration of creative genius. In a remarkable little volume, *Song and Its Foun-*

tains,[14] George Russell, the Irish poet, has written an absorbingly interesting analysis of the psychological origin of some of his best known poems. One gets from the inside of the poet's mind an account of the sources of poetic inspiration. Many of them he traces to the dreams and visions of childhood in which "Earth revealed itself to me as a living being, and rock and clay were made transparent so that I saw lordlier and lovelier beings than I had known before and was made partner in memories of mighty things, happening in ages long sunken behind time. . . ." I have found, he says, "this duality in every thing in my life and I can only surmise some wisdom above the outworn eager heart, which understands that we cannot be wholly of this world or wholly of the heaven world and we cannot enter that Deity out of which came good and evil, light and darkness, spirit and matter, until our being is neither one or the other, but a fusion of opposites a unity akin to the Fullness, when spirit, desire and substance are raised above themselves and exist in that mystic unity of all things which we call Deity."

Here speaks a poet who has given thought to the sources of his own poetic vision and finds that it comes from a self that transcends the conscious self. For him poetic insight arises from the dreams of childhood when earth revealed itself as a living being, before the barriers of the self-conscious mind had raised themselves between his soul and the soul of all. It is just this identification of the inner and the outer self, the interpenetration of object and subject that one feels in Van Gogh's art. The religious fervor of his youth was carried over into the fanatic zeal of his painting. In his soul he felt the travail of all creation. The distorted forms and the frenzied use of color were the expressions of a spiritual necessity to communicate his message of a world alive, suffering, violent, and yet a world in which an all-atoning

[14] *Song and Its Fountains,* George Russell, The Macmillan Company, New York, 1932.

love revealed itself in the tragic beauty of the commonplace.

Thus we find in the psychoanalytic concept of the unconscious an account of dreams and symbols, the myths and folklore of the primitive, the phantasies of the neurotic, the instinctive drives, the patterns of life and behavior inherited from past generations—all of these extending in time beyond the consciousness of the present moment, and functioning in a hundred different ways in normal human behavior. From this grows the conscious ego, an organic unity, experienced as unique and separate, but nevertheless one with the environment which supports it and to which it reacts.

More than this, while the unconscious may be the seat of madness, it is also the source of creative genius. In its creative function it is the intuitive awareness of realities that have not yet reached the level of conscious experience. The vision of the poet, the form and color which exist first in the psyche of the artist, the as yet unheard melodies of the composer, and the "hunch" of the inventor, all come from that part of the mind that extends beyond the limits of consciousness. If we think of the creativeness of genius as the thrust of the evolutionary drive in man, then we may speak of the unconscious as containing not only the drive of the past, but the pull of the future in human evolution. In it man's origin and man's destiny meet. The drag of the spirit's past weighs down its flight into the future, and that endless conflict between the self that *is* and the self that *would be* is waged in the subliminal depths of the unconscious. In the conflict arises that sense of guilt and sin from which man seeks atonement, and from it, too, arises that vision of the savior whose suffering and triumph brings freedom and salvation.

If we give a constructive interpretation to the teachings of psychology, we find in them a conception of human personality that unites it in organic union with the material world from which it has evolved and also points toward the unfolding of the psyche in a world of spiritual values. The very existence of the nervous mechanism, through which conditioned behavior is effected and the necessary organic responses are automatically elicited without the expenditure of psychical energy, leaves the higher centers of the brain free for the creative activities of the intellect and the intuition. The possibility of a collective unconscious unites the whole human family in a psychical unity that overleaps the barriers of nationality, color and race, and betokens a solidarity that is an essential reality rather than the expression of benevolent sentiment. The sense of individual isolation is not man's highest or final recognition of himself and of his own significance. Faith in the slowly dawning consciousness of the human spirit as an organic unity that, by the long and painful process of evolution, is externalizing the spiritual Will and Purpose of a living Universe—this, it seems, is not incompatible with the trend of constructive thought in modern psychology.

Chapter 8

Christianity and Human Evolution

"What I want to achieve, what I have been striving and pining to achieve these thirty years, is self-realization—to see God face to face, to attain salvation."

Mohandas K. Gandhi[1]

"Christianity, being realistic, conceives that knowledge has a dynamic object, the world which the mind does not misrepresent altogether; but may describe more and more justly. For the world was made by God who has a mind after which our own minds were fashioned."

George Santayana[2]

"Jesus as a concrete historical personality remains a stranger to our time, but his spirit which lies hidden in his words is known in simplicity and its influence is direct."

Albert Schweitzer[3]

We return from the rather long detour on the roads of science and psychology to resume our attempt at a stereoscopic view of modern science and Christian faith from the standpoint of religion. The reader may have felt that he was being taken pretty far afield from the subject in hand, but there was a method in the author's madness. His purpose was two-fold—first to bring out the fact that science itself does not accept its solutions as either complete or final. It builds up a theoretical framework in which to correlate the scientific facts of today, only to rebuild and revise this frame-

1 *Gandhi's Autobiography*. Public Affairs Press, Washington, D.C., 1948.
2 *The Idea of Christ in the Gospel*: Charles Scribner's Sons, New York, 1940.
3 *The Quest of the Historical Jesus*: A. and C. Black, Ltd., London, 1946.

work to accommodate the new and possibly contradictory facts of tomorrow's discoveries. The working scientist is not nearly so sure of the permanence of his concepts and theories as the layman uninitiated in the tricks of the scientist's trade might suppose. A further purpose of our scientific side trip was to try to show how the expanding world of scientific thought has led to an increasing necessity to integrate our ideas of the physical and the spiritual in order to reach a clearer conception of the conscious human being and his relation to his total environment. In short we were looking at science from a religious point of view.

We have now to tackle the other half of our job of getting a stereoscopic vision of the scientific and the religious by looking at the essentials of Christian faith with the same intellectual detachment as that with which we would scrutinize an economic theory or a philosophy of history. This is by long odds the harder part of the undertaking and the writer can promise only an honest attempt to transcend his own individual bias as one who has a "will to believe."

At the very outset we face the serious problem of deciding just what are the essential elements of Christian faith. As had been noted, early Christianity absorbed many alien elements from contemporary cults that are not to be found in the simple teachings of its founder or in the beliefs of its earliest adherents. These alien elements have been incorporated not only in the dogmas of the institutionalized Christianity, but more deeply implanted in the unconscious lives of Christians by the symbolism and ritual of religious practices. There is the further difficulty arising from the fact that the content of Christian thought and feeling is not something carved out of experience by the intellect, but is rather a living thing whose roots are buried in the emotional depth of millions of lives throughout the centuries, and whose branches extend far into the social, cultural and religious institutions of the civilization with which it has grown. Its tremendous vitality, like that of a great tree in a tropical forest, has fed a multitude of parasitic growths that partake of its vital energy but are not essential elements of its organic life.

From its inception the Christian religion began to absorb many lasting elements in its body of belief and practices from sources other than the simple teachings of its founder. Hebrew monotheism and Greek metaphysics went into its intellectual content and the mystery cults of the East contributed to its mystical and emotional elements. Later in its history, the imperialism of ancient Rome found its way into the ecclesiastical empire of the medieval Church. Christian scholarship has devoted a vast amount of painstaking historical and critical research to tracing the sources and influences of the many tributary streams whose confluence produced the mighty river of Christian thought and feeling whose waters have fed the spiritual life of Western civilization.

The religion of Jesus came into being at a moment of history and under a concurrence of cultural, religious and political conditions that were peculiarly favorable to its widespread acceptance throughout the ancient world. Two widely divergent explanations of the historic facts are possible. Seen from the interior point of view the combination of circumstances and events that marked the beginning of the Christian era and promoted the marvelous growth and survival of Christianity among a multitude of competing cults has been interpreted as evidence of its divine origin. The believer explains it all by saying that God chose this particularly favorable moment in history for the revelation of himself in the person of Jesus of Nazareth as a part of the Divine plan for human redemption. The believer invokes the supernatural in his explanation of an historical event.

Secular thought on the other hand finds no element of the supernatural in the historic facts. Given the world conditions of the period and the natural religious proclivities of man and a new religion will naturally arise. As a matter of fact a number of them did. Such is the nature of the human creature that new religions are always emerging. The fact that Christianity spread throughout the then civilized world is no more evidence of its supernatural origin than is the equally phenomenal rise of Islam through the Syrian world some six centuries later. That it was Christianity which survived the collapse of Graeco-Roman civilization rather than Mithraism, its nearest rival, argues nothing more, says the sceptic, than its superior fitness to survive in the then existing cultural environment.

To ascribe a wholly supernatural origin to Christianity immediately places it beyond scientific explanation. Such a belief, argues the sceptical mind, presupposes an acceptance of the fundamental assumptions of the religion that the facts of its origin are supposed to support. "If," says the sceptic, "you accept those assumptions as valid, then you don't need to bring any supernatural elements into its origin to strengthen your belief in what you have already assumed." This would seem to be perfectly sound logic, and the situation apparently resolves itself into a question of a choice between the logic of the sceptic and the faith of the believer.

Now it should be noted that the sceptic's position is ultimately grounded in his "will to believe" no less than is that of the believer. To be sure what the sceptic believes is superficially only the antithesis of the believer's faith in the existence of the supernatural. He sees religious phenomena as entirely natural phenomena that can be explained in naturalistic, that is to say humanistic, terms without the unnecessary assumption of the existence of God or of any purpose of God in human history. Obviously we have here in our attempt to interpret historic facts a situation involving two mutually contradictory ideas. To adopt one seems automatically to exclude the other.

This presents the same sort of dilemma as are the dilemmas which physical facts continually present to the scientist.

We propose to follow in the present instance a procedure that has full scientific sanction and maintain that an explanation of the facts of Christian origins can be found in the operation of a process that is at the same time both natural and supernatural. Whether this procedure will pass the test of being orthodox science or being orthodox religion may be questioned, but progress and orthodoxy in either science or religion seldom dwell together in comfort under one ideological roof. And after all the formulations of the finite minds of either scientists or theologians are not final or sacrosanct.

The scientific view of the origin and meaning of Christianity involves nothing more radical than an interpretation of the facts in evolutionary terms. Without discarding the traditional religious view, we may see the same set of facts and circumstances as an extension into human history of the process which for biological science accounts for the mysterious proliferation of life in the organic world. Traditional theology sees the introduction of Christian thought and ideals into the stream of human history as the supreme act in the dramatic story of man's fall and redemption, as set forth in the Hebraic-Christian scripture. We may equally well see the fact from the point of view of modern science as marking a mutation in the evolution of the spiritual side of man's nature. The merging of the two views should give a more complete realization of the meaning of the mystery of Existence itself. The full glory of a diamond is revealed only when one sees it from more than a single angle of vision.

Scientific description represents the natural world in terms of a creative evolutionary process in which evidences of purpose, as opposed to blind chance, can be found. To accept either purpose or chance in explanation of the order in nature revealed by science is a matter of belief. We may accept the former as a perfectly tenable scientific hypothesis, recognizing that the ideas of both purpose and chance are meaningless apart from conscious experience. Since in the very nature of things all that we can say about man's world must be expressed in human terms, we leave the question of purpose in the cosmos as a whole to the speculations of the philosophers. So far as we mortals are concerned we need only think of the process of purposive evolution as beginning with that minor cosmic event that left our tiny planet so favorably placed with reference to the radiant energy from its parent star. By "favorable" we mean conducive to life as we know it on our globe.

This purposive process can be seen as continuing throughout those millions of years of geological history in which a glowing cinder was transformed into a nurturing mother for the life that was to emerge from it. We see it too in the provision of the outer envelope of water, carbon dioxide, oxygen and nitrogen that the chief constituents both of living organisms and the environment that sustains them. Its creative aspect appears in the emergence of that greatest of all scientific mysteries, the living cell, and equally in the expanding series of biological mutations which in the course of millions of years have produced the myriads of species that comprise the world of organic nature.

Science does not see the whole evolutionary process as a single sequence of events purposefully directed toward a single goal. The scientific picture is rather that of a boundless vital urge that expresses itself in adaptive variations in existing forms and in radical divergences from those forms—mutations that, under the sifting action of environmental factors, may or may not survive as enduring species. The order in organic nature appears as a multitude of purposes. The goal in any particular case is a species that is fitted to survive in the environment in which it has evolved. Life does not present itself as a static state of being, but rather as a continuing process of becoming, in which birth and death, growth and decay are the up and down beats in the rhythm of existence.

Although evolution as a whole does not appear as purposefully directed to a single end, yet it does in certain cases exhibit an extended line of variations and mutations that, after the event, can rationally be interpreted as the quest of a definite goal. Such a sequence does not appear as a series of events each of which occurs as the necessary result of antecedent causes. It may be interpreted rather as one might interpret the unity that is found in the artistic creation of a great symphony. Starting with a single theme, the composer works out upon it a series of variations. Having developed its musical possibilities, he suddenly introduces a new theme, an act of artistic creation. The new appears not as caused by the old, but as the development of the over-all creative purpose of the composer. The unity and beauty of the entire symphonic movement emerge from the synthesis of the new and the old. The whole is greater than the sum of its parts.

In scientific terms, the idea of what has been called "evolution in a straight line" goes under the name of "orthogenesis". It applies to those cases in which a succession of minor variations, together with marked divergences from existing forms, mutations, have a cumulative effect in a combination of characters that give to the evolved species outstanding fitness to survive in the existing environment. Biological science has no explanation in its own terms to offer as to how orthogenesis occurs, and there is divided opinion as to whether it is even a tenable scientific hypothesis. But to ascribe those cases in nature in which it *seems* to have occurred to pure chance would be an expression of a belief not unlike that of a foolish gambler who expects the repeated throws of an honest set of dice to turn up consistently combinations that would make him an unfailing winner. The contrary belief that evolution is "not a chapter of accidents" but that its operation in nature may be interpreted as an expression of purpose is an entirely rational attitude to take.

The second point we would make in our synthesis of

scientific description and Christian faith is this: that the long line of evolutionary development on the basic pattern of the mammalian vertebrates through the order of the primates, the common ancestral stock of man and his anthropoid cousins, can reasonably be considered as an outstanding example of orthogenesis. In this view the evolution of the human species is not regarded as a chapter of accidents with man as its concluding paragraph, but as the expression of a continuing purpose directed toward a definite end. The end of that line of evolutionary development is a species that has demonstrated its fitness to survive under any and all of the vast variations in natural environment that are to be found on this earth. Development took place in the direction of a larger and more highly organized brain, an endowment which man shares with the orangutan and the gorilla, his close animal relatives. But beyond this point in the evolutionary process there emerged in genus *homo* a set of new, unexplained and scientifically unexplainable uniquely human characters. Regarded as an animal man has a decidedly second-rate equipment for survival in almost any kind of environment. From a mechanical point of view his anatomical structure is a very poor piece of engineering. The suspension of his viscera from his spinal column is a particularly bad bit of design in a creature who insists upon going on two legs rather than on all fours. Naturally, he can neither swim nor climb a tree. His lack of a hairy covering would confine his natural habitat to the warm region of the tropics. With nothing more than his purely animal inheritance he would long since have become as extinct as the dodo. In and of itself the possession of a large brain would have had no survival value.

But with that large brain there appeared something entirely new in the process of evolution, one of those tremendous "leaps of nature" scientifically as mysterious as is the origin of life. It was only with the emergence of those distinctly human characters — consciousness of self, intelligence, the ability to employ present means to future ends, memory and foresight, the social as opposed to the individualistic instinct for self-preservation, the mental capacity to invent language—it was with these that man, the inferior animal, became "fit to survive" in the world of nature from which he evolved. As a spiritual being, man can only be regarded as a mutation, a sharply decisive break in the course of the evolution that produced him. The *mind* of man can be regarded as the result of an act of pure creation—something new in the totality of organic life. Science has no explanation in its own terms to offer for the existence of the human mind. Christian faith ascribes it to the creative Will of God. The finite spirit of man is the developing image of the infinite Spirit of man's Creator.

As a final consideration in the synthesis of the opposing ideas of a natural versus a supernatural origin and meaning of Christianity, we carry the evolutionary account of man's creation over into the field of human history. It is entirely reasonable to assume that a process that has gone on through the whole history of the earth should not stop with the appearance of even so remarkable a creature as the human biped. From his own point of view man is the center and crown of all creation, but even so, his insistent striving for new goals is evidence that he is not satisfied with the present end result of his own evolution. The evolutionary drive is still operating within him. As has been suggested, the scientific urge and the religious impulse are two expressions of this element of his nature. His progress from savagery to civilization is a continuation, but with a radical divergence in direction, of his biological evolution. There is little evidence of any significant variation in his physical constitution during the last two hundred thousand years. Evolution in man is proceeding in the development of those distinctively human qualities that set him apart as something radically different from his animal ancestry.

Just as in biological evolution, the story of mankind is

not the record of an unbroken onward and upward march of progress. It appears rather as one of trial and error, success and failure, progressions and retrogressions. Man's gregarious instincts lead to the social organisms of the family, the communal life of the savage tribe, the loosely-organized barbarous state and the formation of nations and empires. With these have grown many diverse cultures and civilizations. Some of them have flourished and grown to the climax of greatness only to decline and die. In his monumental *Study of History* Arnold Toynbee has given us a dramatic picture of this process going on during the six thousand years of recorded history. He sees the rise and fall of empires, the creations and disintegrations of historic societies as the ebb and flow of a life force, the evolutionary drive in the spiritual nature of man. In his view, elaborated with a wealth of detail, civilizations arise in the response of the human spirit to the challenge of adverse conditions that can only be met by the exercise of the latent creative powers of man's nature. According to Toynbee, the true interpretation of the great movements in history is to be stated in spiritual rather than in biological terms.

We supplement this view in our synthesis of the religious and scientific conceptions of the origin of Christianity with the proposition that the centuries of prior religious development from which Christianity ultimately emerged can be quite properly considered an example of orthogenesis in man's spiritual evolution. Seen in the light of history, the twenty centuries of the life of ancient Israel, during which the tribal Jahveh of a nomadic tribe was transformed into an ethical God of justice and mercy, can be regarded as an evolutionary process operating toward a definite end. The parallel intellectual rise in Greek thought that led to the conception of God as a necessary postulate in a philosophical explanation of the world of men and things can be seen as operating to the same end. The development of the ideas of a redemptive sacrifice of a god and of personal salvation through mystical union of the soul of the believer with the god himself that appeared in the mystery cults evidences a widespread psychological approach to the central idea that animated early Christianity.

Finally, there is the fact that these streams of religious, intellectual and psychological influences converged in a disintegrating civilization at a time when the souls of men were seeking for security in a religious faith of hope and salvation. One may, of course, regard all these as accidents whose concurrence proved favorable to the origin and growth of one of the great religions of the world. We believe that they may be interpreted more rationally as the operation of purpose in the evolution of the spiritual side of man's nature. Just as the emergence of the human mind gave to primitive man the means of survival as an animal, so the emergence of those moral and religious ideals that found living expression in the personality of Jesus of Nazareth made for the survival and growth of spiritual powers of man's nature, which, in the continuing process of human evolution, will insure his survival in the face of those self-destructive instincts that stem from his animal origin.

The foregoing extension of the idea of purposive evolution to include the historic facts of the origin of Christianity effects, for the writer at least, a synthesis of the natural and the supernatural explanation of those facts. The historic event that marks the initial date of the Christian calendar was the humble birth of a child in a little town in an obscure province of the Roman Empire. In the soul of that child grown to manhood there arose to the level of human consciousness an Idea, a spiritual reality. In evolutionary terms the emergence of that Idea can be seen as an expression of creative purpose. Its origin is beyond scientific explanation in exactly the same way as are the origins of Life, and the origin of the mind of man as a function of the human brain. The expression in one perfect human life of the Idea of God in Man is both natural and supernatural in the same way as are the origins of Life and Mind. The mystery of the Incarnation is of a piece with the supreme mystery of all existence.

Now it must be recognized that the Christian dogma of the Incarnation is a theological formulation that came many years after the historic fact of the life of the central figure of the Christian faith. It arose, as will be pointed out later, in a philosophical interpretation of the traditional accounts of the life and teachings of Jesus, and the widely accepted belief in his miraculous birth and resurrection in terms of then-current metaphysical concepts. The human personality in whom the Idea was incarnate appears to us in vague and shadowy outlines.

We see Him as one shrouded in the mists of the past, with a mystical light of revelation shining about his head, but with his face half-concealed in the shadow. It is not the man Jesus that is seen with the eye of faith, but rather the mysterious figure of the Christ, the revelation of God in human flesh.

In the words of Albert Schweitzer, he appears as the "prime example of that antithesis between spiritual and natural truth that underlies all life and all events, and in Him emerges into the field of history." Again in the words of Schweitzer, "the early Christians have handed down to us, no biographies of Jesus, but only Gospels, and therefore we possess the Idea and the Person with the minimum of historical and contemporary limitations."[4]

However, a scientifically objective approach to the problem of the antithesis of the natural and the spiritual in the origin of Christianity demands that we try to look at the recorded facts in the life of its founder with the same degree of detachment with which we would regard any historical record. Unfortunately for this purpose the accounts of those facts are matters of tradition and legend. Moreover, they bear evidence of having been written years after the events

[4] *The Quest of the Historical Jesus*: A. and C. Black, Ltd., London, 1946.

which they chronicle as propaganda for the promotion of the new religion. The form in which they finally emerged is the New Testament, containing the four Gospel stories of the life and ministry of Jesus, the Acts of the Apostles, twenty-one letters ascribed to the Apostles and addressed to the religious groups in various parts of the Roman world, and the apocalyptic Book of Revelation. Aside from internal evidence nothing is certainly known of the exact dates or the circumstances of their writing. They were established by the organized Church as the canonical Scripture about the year 350 A.D. We are told that before the year 120 A.D. no reference is made to the four Gospels in the writings of the early Christian fathers. Scholars are agreed that none of the narrative accounts of the life of Jesus could have been written earlier than forty years after his death. The first reference to the Christians in Roman history occurs no earlier than 117 A.D., when Tacitus wrote that the Emperor Nero had subjected them to cruel torture. He states that "Christ, from whom they took their name, had been put to death under Tiberius by the Procurator, Pontius Pilate."

Perhaps no single event in recorded history has ever received more intensive research than Christian scholarship has devoted to the Gospel narratives of the life of Jesus of Nazareth. In the four Gospels we have four accounts of the life and the works of this remarkable personage whose preaching and teaching were accompanied by miracles of healing and, according to some of the accounts, of restoring the dead to life. Two of the Gospels relate miraculous events accompanying his birth. All report his crucifixion, death, and his subsequent appearance on a number of occasions to his followers. The earliest reference to his life from an external source is that of Flavius Josephus (37-94 A.D.), a Hellenized Jew, who speaks of Jesus as a "wise man, who accomplished marvelous things," who was put to death by Pilatus at the instigation of the elders of the Jewish people, who charged him with being the leader of an abortive insurrection against the Roman government. (This last is taken from a recently re-discovered translation in Old Russian of Josephus' *History of the Jewish War*. The authenticity of this document is questioned by some scholars.)

The first three, the Synoptic Gospels, record the teachings and the miracles of Jesus. The introduction of the Gospel of Luke indicates that numerous accounts were extant of those things which were taught and believed among the later members of the sect. There are in the three accounts many exact agreements in wording which indicate that they were in part at least derived from a common earlier source, while at the same time there are important differences which might well arise from the fact that portions of the accounts came from oral tradition, with the inevitable resulting variations in details. But more than this, there are certain outright contradictions, such as the two conflicting genealogies given in Matthew and Luke, both purporting to trace Jesus' descent from King David, through Joseph; a still further contradiction, since both accounts describe his miraculous conception, hence his human genealogy could only be traced through his mother.

If, as radical scepticism maintains, the whole story is a legend and a myth, it was not a "*cunningly* devised fable", for any degree of cleverness on the part of the devisers could most certainly have avoided such palpable discrepancies. The most that can be said for the records of the first three Gospels, regarded simply as history, is that they give us what must be regarded as at best hearsay accounts of the life and works of a great religious teacher. He is represented as teaching no formal doctrine, but as imparting the truth of his message in parables suited to the understanding of the multitudes of the poor and simple folk who followed him to hear his message and for the sake of the miracles which he performed. He is represented as coming to his death through the enmity which he aroused among the priestly and rabbinical classes. In his public references to himself he makes no claims either to his Messiah-ship or to his divinity, but always speaks of himself as the "Son of Man". Only among his followers is the secret of his Messiah-ship disclosed, and that by implication, rather than by direct statement.

His teachings parallel those of the Hebrew prophets in their ethical content, in their insistence upon justice, mercy and righteousness. They differ in the emphasis that he places upon the spirit of love which must animate human relations, as opposed to the formalistic observance of prescribed ceremonial. Finally throughout his teaching, as recorded in the Synoptic Gospels, is the insistent, ever-recurring strain of a God of love, who marks the fall of the sparrow and clothes the lilies of the field in beauty, and whose relation to man is that of a father to his children. He teaches his disciples when they pray to say "Our Father, who art in heaven," and speaks to them of God as "your Father". He refers to God as his own Father, but without any implication as to the uniqueness of his sonship, save in the keen intensity of his own awareness of this intimate relationship. His teachings are marked by his deep conviction of their truth. He is described as one speaking "with authority and not as the scribes". His code of ethics, contained in the direct, simple injunctions of the Sermon on the Mount is based on the broad fundamentals of love of God, and love of one's fellow men. His conception of the Kingdom of God is that of an other-worldly kingdom, a living thing, having its roots in the hearts of men.

Repeated references indicate that at certain times he entertained the thought of the coming of the Kingdom as something which would occur in the near future, and of himself as its central figure. Later, he foresaw his own death at the instigation of the leaders of his people and foretold his resurrection and his second coming to usher in the Kingdom of God. Filled with love and tender compassion for the poor and the suffering, he uttered the most bitter denunciation of the religious leaders of his time, "who devoured widows' houses, and, for a pretence, made long prayers." The Gospels record that he was seized by these leaders, given an ecclesiastical trial, found guilty of blasphemy and judged worthy of death. Brought before the Roman governor he was accused of inciting insurrection by having made claims to being King of the Jews. Yielding to the tumult of the mob, Pilate ordered his crucifixion. All of the Gospels record, with varying and somewhat conflicting details, his appearance to his disciples after his death and burial. Biblical scholars differ widely in their judgments of the authenticity of the texts describing the resurrection, but all are agreed that implicit belief in a risen Lord, and in his early second coming to establish the Kingdom of God on earth, was the dynamic drive which animated his early disciples and led to the rapid rise of Christianity in the first two centuries of the Christian era.

Thus we have in outline a traditional account of the teachings of the central figure of Christianity as recorded in ancient texts of whose freedom from subsequent interpolations we are far from certain. Leaving aside the matter of the supernatural events that purportedly accompanied his birth and death, we have the picture of one possessed by visions of a world of possibilities which were soon to be realized in the Kingdom of God. A Jew, his visions were seen against a background of Jewish tradition. That tradition was of one God who was righteous and demanded the obedience of his chosen people, of a God who was concerned with what men do, and who had revealed his will in the law and through the prophets. Supplementing their idea of God as the lawgiver was the later Jewish conception of God as merciful and full of compassion for the frailties and sinfulness of men, a God whose forgiveness was freely granted to those who turned to him in true repentance. The Old Testament Scriptures are replete with expressions of the loving kindness of God. These portions of the Judaistic faith have been taken over completely by Christian teaching. Quoting the words of

Professor Goodenough, "In keeping the Old Testament as at first its only sacred Scriptures, and in never abandoning the Jewish Scriptures, even after its own New Testament was formed, Christianity has publicly proclaimed itself the successor, the consummation, of Judaism. . . . In their deepest moments of religion, Christians pray in the words of forgotten Jews."[5]

Reading the narratives of the first three Gospels, we note two facts that stand out in bold relief as new and unique and not to be accounted for by Jesus' training in the faith of his people. The first was the deep, unalterable conviction of his own intimate personal relation with God, the Father. How otherwise could any but a madman speak with the absolute authority with which his utterances are clothed. The second is the equally deep conviction that through his own person was to be realized the Kingdom of God whose coming he foresaw. The record indicates that in the early stages of his preaching he cherished the hope that through his teaching and wonder-working he could achieve the mighty work. Later, with the growing opposition from the established order, he realized that this would not come to pass. Deep in his unconscious, perhaps, was the symbol of redemption, the age-old idea of salvation through sacrifice. Impelled by this new vision he resolutely left the safety of his Galilean hillsides, and with his disciples resolutely turned his face to Jerusalem, where he foresaw that his enemies would put him to death. It was in his sublime faith in God, his Father, and in the certain coming of the Kingdom of God, that he foretold his resurrection. In the story of his Passion, the agony in the Garden of Gethsemane, one sees the record of the struggle between the will of a man to live, the survival instinct, and the drive of a supreme idea, stronger than the love of life itself. In the narratives of the cruel scenes of the trial and the slow torture of the crucifixion,

[5] *Religious Tradition and Myth,* E. R. Goodenough, Yale University Press, 1937.

the figure of the Galilean mystic moves serenely triumphant to the accomplishment of his great mission. Nowhere in history nor in literature do we find a nobler picture of the triumph of the spirit over the bitter humiliation of apparent defeat and the physical torture of a cruel death than is given in the direct, simple Gospel accounts of the passion and death of Jesus. To accept it as only legend and myth, a pure figment of human imagination, calls for greater credulity than to believe it as an historical fact. The account lacks all evidence of poetic embellishment or the symbolic language of mythology. Its stark simplicity stamps it as a record of fact, rather than a creation of fancy.

The Cross thus became the symbol of Christian faith. For countless thousands down through the centuries it has stood not only as a reminder of the suffering and death of the founder of their faith but as a sure token of man's salvation through suffering. In any account which we give of the origin of Christianity, we shall miss its profoundest meaning if we neglect the psychological fact that deep in the unconscious of the race is imbedded the belief that redemption comes only through suffering. Sacrifice, the giving of the best for the salvation of all, appears in every expression of the religious impulse. It is symbolized in the bloody rites of savage worship, and finds expression in the central dogma of Christian theology, the doctrine of the Atonement. It has frequently been urged that the story of the Cross is only another version of a primitive superstition, based upon the sadistic instincts of the savage mind. It may with equal cogency be maintained that its universal appeal marks it as meeting a deep-rooted need of the psychical life of the race.

There is an important difference to be noted in the story of the Cross as told in the Synoptic Gospels from the idea of atonement as it is set forth in pagan mythology and in Jewish theology. In these latter the victim is sacrificed as a means of placating an angry or an outraged deity. Throughout Christian history, the suffering and death of Jesus have been pictured as an expiatory act to meet the demands of justice. Man has sinned, and has violated God's law. His guilt can only be expunged, the demands of a righteous God can only be met by punishment. "Without the shedding of blood there is no remission." In the old ceremonial law the killing of a lamb, the firstling of the flock without spot or blemish, symbolized the sacrifice that was necessary. The Feast of the Atonement, the high point of the Jewish ceremonial year, celebrated this rite. Thus to the mind of the Jewish disciples of Jesus, the most natural interpretation of the death of their Lord was that of the fulfilment of the ancient ceremonial law. In the writings of Paul we find it carried over into the theological teachings of Christianity, and it is expressed in the language of the Eucharist. Much of the evangelistic preaching today and many hymns of the church are expressions of this idea of the atonement of sin by the expiatory death of Jesus. What was a natural belief for the mind of nineteen centuries ago has been carried down through the ages, and when stated in these primitive terms is repulsive in the highest degree to our modern ideas of justice.

But if we go to the accounts of the Synoptic Gospels, we see the suffering and death of Jesus not as a sacrificial act to appease the wrath of an angry God, but rather as a deliberately chosen means for the realization of his vision of the Kingdom of God.

It is difficult to see before the event what possible connection might have been made in the mind of Jesus between his death and the coming of the Kingdom of God. In the cold light of reason it appears as the mad act of a religious fanatic. As a matter of history, the expected catastrophic end of the existing order and the return of the Son of Man did not occur. What did occur was the rise of a new religion whose central fact was the death of its founder, and this death was interpreted in terms of the Jewish idea of sacrificial atonement.

But this interpretation of Jesus' death, taken over from Judaism and adopted by the early Christian church, departs radically from the meaning given to it in the Synoptic Gospels. Nowhere in Jesus' recorded utterances do we find any trace of the conception of an angry God whose wrath was to be averted by the suffering and death of an innocent victim. In his thought, God was the forgiving Father of the parable of the prodigal son, who saw the penitent "when he was still a great way off" and had compassion on him. His prayer on the Cross for his tormentors, "Father, forgive them; they know not what they do," is the expression of a divine pity for the blind ignorance of sin.

In the light of Jesus' own words, as transmitted in the first three Gospels, we can see his death not as a means of satisfying the demands of Divine Justice, but rather as a revelation of Divine Love.

Interpreting the rise of Christianity as the expression of a plan pre-formed in the mind of God, we are baffled in our attempt to reconcile two such diverse conceptions of the central fact of its origin. Looking at it as a fact of supreme significance in man's spiritual evolution, the emergence of a new character in the conscious life of the race, we can understand how the old and the emergent strains might persist together as, indeed, they have even to the present moment.

Thought of in evolutionary terms, Christianity may be considered as an emergent synthesis of three distinct elements: the ethical monotheism of the Jews, the philosophical idealism of Greek Platonism, and the creative conception, in the mind of Jesus of Nazareth, of *love* as the creative principle, whose expression in human terms is the coming of the Kingdom of God. Seen in this light, it is not surprising that we should find diverse and even contradictory elements. The fusion is not yet complete. Primitive Christianity was overburdened with the Hebrew contribution. Medieval scholasticism struggled with the impossible task of a purely rational synthesis of the intellectual content of the three elements. Modern Christian scholorship has made a valiant but vain attempt at rational reconciliation of the divergent strains by the methods of critical analysis.

Jesus' vision of the catastrophic arrival of the Kingdom of God has given place to our modern conception of the growth of a creative idea. His death was the supreme dramatization of a fundamental law of human life—that the spiritual evolution of the race, the emancipation of man from his animal heritage, must be paid for by the voluntary sacrifice of the noblest for the realization of the vision of a better world. The deepest significance of his resurrection is not in his personal appearance to his Galilean followers, but rather in the appearance of his spirit and the power of his example in the lives of those thousands of lesser saviors of the race whose lives are the ever-living expression of their faith, and whose devotion to the realization of the vision of the Kingdom of God gives vital meaning to the symbol of the Cross, and a profound significance to the story of the Resurrection.

While the idea of a redeeming Messiah and of his sacrificial atonement for sin, of which the Jewish mind was so acutely conscious, had a powerful appeal to religious Jews dispersed throughout the Roman Empire, yet it was a conception entirely foreign to the rational-minded Greeks dispersed throughout the Empire, and equally so to the practical-minded Romans. What was there inherent in the new religion, or what interpretation might be given of its teachings, which appealed to these latter in whom the natural religious impulse was almost as strong as in the Jews?

It was through the tremendous missionary zeal of Paul, the Apostle to the Gentiles, that primitive Christianity broke over the barriers of Judaism and offered itself to the world. If we study his writings with reference to the background of religious belief prevailing among the religious-minded of his Greek hearers, I think we will find that it is his conception of the mystical union of the soul of the believer with Christ, the Redeemer, that made the most powerful appeal to them.

Traditionally, the Greeks had always thought of the gods as personally and intimately related to human affairs. In Homer they are represented as taking sides and playing favorites in the quarrels and warfare of men. Along with this humanistic idea were numerous cults of Eastern origin, pantheistic in spirit, yet emphasizing the conception of the unity of the soul with the god, and picturing the body as a prison house from which the soul was freed in the mystical rites of initiation into the cult. To minds so conditioned, Paul's teachings of a rebirth of the soul, a mystic communion with Christ, and of a life after death in which the spirit was freed from the fetters of the flesh, all held powerful emotional appeal. It is impossible to say to what extent the profound psychological experience of the Apostle's own conversion is to be referred to these mystical conceptions of the Greek mind which are so foreign to the Jewish temper. It is equally impossible to evaluate their influence upon his interpretation of the inner meaning of Jesus' life and teaching. But viewing the whole matter of the origin of Christianity from the point of view of emergent evolution, as the creative synthesis of existing elements into a new whole which is more than the sum of its parts, we can get a far deeper sense of its significance than by an after-the-fact analysis of the antecedent conditions from which it emerged.

Looking backward in history to the origin of Christianity, it is easy to find its individual elements in the pre-existing conditions of Greek and Jewish religious thought. But just as it is impossible to account for the properties of water from all that we can possibly know of its constituent elements, hydrogen and oxygen, before their actual synthesis, so it is equally impossible to account for the tremendous vitality of Christianity in terms of the antecedent facts of earlier religions. Judaism was inexorably bound within racial limits. It was not evangelical. The Greek cults were limited in their appeal and decidedly on the wane at the beginning of our era. The synthesis of these by means of what, to continue our chemical analogy, we may call the catalytic action of the traditional account of the life and death of Jesus of Nazareth, resulted in a new movement in the spiritual evolution of man, a religion that knew no boundaries or race or color, in which there was "neither Jew nor Greek, neither bond nor free."

From the Greek slave it spread like a contagion into the household of his Roman master. In two centuries the number of its converts and its undermining influence on official paganism made Christianity a major problem of Roman domination. Within three centuries we find the Emperor Constantine seeking the support of his Christian subjects and giving Christianity a privileged position in the Empire. In less than another century pagan sacrifices were prohibited by imperial edict. At the beginning of the fifth century pagans were forbidden to hold public office. Christianity as an organized religion had triumphed. Its history from the fifth century on merged with that of the Church. From there on the pure waters of its spiritual origin became a part of the turbid mighty stream of the political, social and ecclesiastical life of the Middle Ages.

We have tried to present an elementary picture of the psychological interaction between the new religion and its Hebrew and Greek religious antecedents, an interrelation that was a potent factor in its promulgation, and a powerful influence in forming its body of belief. An equally important fact is to be found in the purely intellectual contributions of speculative thought to Christian dogma. The Judaistic conception of the supreme Being combined the ideas of God as the creator of the world and as the righteous lawgiver. Christianity incorporated these elements in its conception of the Deity. The high point of Greek philosophical thought on the other hand was the Platonic view of God as the Absolute Mind, the seat of the eternal Ideas of which temporal and physical realities are the transient images. The Jewish conception was concrete, definite and particular. The Greek was abstract and universal. Neither conception provided any direct avenue of approach of individual consciousness to God. For the Jew, communication was by way of a prescribed ritual under the ministration of the priestcraft. In Plato's philosophy, the only means of approach to the Divine Mind was along the road of pure thought through the abstractions of mathematical reasoning. In both views Deity is conceived of as something apart from and beyond nature, and hence beyond direct human apprehension and contact. The fusion of these two views is to be found in the Christian dogma of the Incarnation. We find it stated very briefly, but very definitely and with the finality of authority, in the prologue to the fourth Gospel. Like the opening measure of Brahms' First Symphony, the author announces his great theme, simple yet profound beyond all understanding. Here we have no truth arrived at by the painful process of logical deduction, or of scientific inference. We accept it either as a supreme truth, or we reject it as the utterance of a religious visionary. As in the opening verses of the book of Genesis, the author goes back to first things.

"In the beginning was the Word (Logos) and the Word was with God, and the Word was God. The same was in the beginning with God. All things were made by him; and without him was not anything made that was made. In him was life, and the life was the light of men. And the light shineth in darkness, and the darkness comprehended it not. . . . That was the true Light, which lighteth every man that cometh into the world. He was in the world, and the world was made by him, and the world knew Him not. He came unto his own, and his own received him not. . . . And the World was made flesh and dwelt among us (and we beheld his glory, the glory as of the only begotten of the Father) full of grace and truth."

These words are an interpretation, expressed in language

that conveyed meaning both to the Jewish and Greek elements of primitive Christianity, of the significance of the life and teachings and death of the vital, dynamic personality in whom their new-found faith was centered. This interpretation was based on both the Old Testament conception of God as the creator of all things and on the philosophic description of God as the Absolute Mind of Greek thought. According to the writer of the book of John, Jesus was both the Messiah of Hebrew expectation and the expression (Logos) in human terms of the Universal Mind of Greek metaphysics.

The account of the Fourth Gospel bears throughout the evidence of this interpretive point of view. Scholars are agreed that it was written much later than the Synoptic Gospels. Even casual comparison with the earlier accounts forces the conclusion that it was an interpretation of events in terms of the propositions stated in the prologue, rather than a narrative of the events themselves. Throughout, Jesus speaks of himself both as the "Son of Man" and, more frequently, as the "Son of God". There are few references to the Kingdom of God and its expected coming. Jesus foretells his death as a redemptive measure ordained and approved by his Father. "Therefore doth my Father love me, because I lay down my life. . . . And I, if I be lifted up, will draw all men unto me." In the figures of the "bread of life," the "water of life," the "light of the world," and in the parable of the good shepherd and the allegory of the vine He is presented as the source of the spiritual life of his followers. His disputes with the religious rulers, as recorded in the first three Gospels, turn almost wholly on matters of observance of the Mosaic Law. In the fourth, the point at issue was predominantly that of the nature and function of Jesus himself—a point on which, in the early church even as today, there was serious disagreement among the philosophically-minded followers of the faith. In other words, the purpose behind the writing of the book of John was an attempted rationalization in philosophical terms of the new truth that had come to the surface of human consciousness through the deeply religious insight of the Galilean carpenter. That truth had of necessity to be expressed in the current conception of the nature of the world, of God, and of man. The very fact that, all down through the centuries of Christian thought, each generation of thinkers has struggled to interpret it in terms of its own particular conceptions of reality, and to set it forth against the background of its own world-view, testifies to its enduring value as a vital element in Christian thought.

It appears as an emergent, a creative, factor in the slow spiritual evolution of the human race—a living thing whose roots go deep into man's past, and whose ever-increasing expression is the supreme hope for man's future.

At this point the critical reader will no doubt observe that the writer has failed in his attempt to maintain an entirely objective attitude toward the subject under discussion. This must be freely admitted. What has just been said is not a statement of scientifically demonstrable fact, but rather a profession of the writer's own religious faith that evolution in the human species is in the direction of the fulfilment of Jesus' vision of the Kingdom of God. Such a faith sees the evil in the world, the hatred, malice, greed and cruelty, as vestiges of humanity's animal origin, accentuated by that sense of isolation which comes from self-consciousness. Feeling himself apart from nature and his fellows, the individual's instinct of self-preservation finds expression in the destruction of that which is feared. Self-assertion, competition, rivalry and war are the overt expression of fear in the human soul.

"Perfect love casteth out fear." The Christian ideal of a God of love and of a Kingdom of God whose law is love is the pull of the future. Christian faith, for the modern mind, is the insight which beholds in the tragedy of the world the travail of an Eternal Spirit of love that is fashioning mankind in its own image in the slow process of human evolution. In such a faith, Jesus the Galilean mystic, who died for the sake of his vision, and the Christ of John's Gospel, the Incarnation of that Eternal Spirit of love, are seen as two expressions of one supreme truth—a truth whose meaning defies statement in the formal terms of the mind, and which can only be validated by the response that it elicits in the hearts and lives of men.

Physical science presents us with an external world of material reality unified in the conceptions of a cosmic *Mind* and a cosmic *Energy*. This is both the universe of science and the God of science, the unconditioned and absolute space-time continuum and the matter-energy unity of electrical wave-particles. The whole course of organic evolution represents the projection of the time axis of the mind-energy of the world as it appears under terrestrial conditions. The psychical nature of man today is the focus of the evolutionary drive in the human species. We have characterized the evolutionary process as an expression of Will and Purpose inherent in the stuff of the world. As an act of rational religious faith we may identify the creative will of the evolutionary process with the Logos of John's gospel. But there is a point of fundamental difference between the two.

In the creative Will, as manifested in the evolutionary drive, there are no ethical or spiritual implications. In Christian teaching the Incarnation of the Logos is a unique personality who is the supreme exemplification of man's finest and noblest ideals of human character. Whatever account we may give of the central figure of Christianity, whether it be that of radical scepticism, or the acceptance of Him as the uniquely divine Son of God, we must admit that the Jesus of Christian tradition stands as the incarnation of the ethical and spiritual grandeur latent in man. "This," says Christian faith, "is the expression in finite human terms of the evolutionary purpose in human history. The world Will, as it is manifested in man's spiritual evolution, is a will to righteousness, justice, mercy and love."

Modern Christian faith, then, is not in opposition to

the world-view of modern science. It can accept all that science has to say about the nature of the world and of man and of God. But it goes further and places the same confidence in the spiritual insight of Jesus that science places in the genius of Newton or Einstein. And that confidence rests upon exactly the same sort of basis in the two cases. The theory of Relativity is not accepted by the scientific mind simply on the authority of a great mathematician. Its acceptance rests upon the fact that other minds can follow the same intellectual processes and arrive at the same intellectual certainty, and upon the fact that its implications can be tested by a certain type of experience known as scientific experiment. Similarly, Jesus' declaration of a God of love can only command acceptance in so far as it can be verified in the inner experience of men and women, and find objective expression in their lives. It must be verified by each individual and by every generation. The truth of Jesus's vision of a loving Father and of a world order ruled by love is attested only by the living faith of those in each generation who have caught the spirit of that vision. If that faith should die out in human hearts, then the story of the man of Galilee, and the whole conception of an effective principle of love operating in human evolution, would have to be relegated to the limbo of myth and outgrown superstition.

The history of the Christian religion and the growth of Western culture are inextricably intertwined. It may be argued that our civilization might have been created without Christianity. As a matter of historic fact it was not. To believe that the ethical, social and political ideals of our democratic way of life could survive the abandonment of the religion with which and out of which it has grown is to ignore the teachings of the history. One needs to go no further back than the period between the two World Wars to find in what happened in Germany an example of how quickly the latent savagery in human nature reasserts itself when the restraints of religion are abandoned.

Christianity was born in an aging civilization whose destruction it survived to become the source of the spiritual life of a new and far greater civilization. It was the humanizing influence that tamed the rude spirits of the barbarous tribes of Western Europe and created the relatively civilized society of medieval feudalism. It was the inspiration of the great art, literature and architecture of the Middle Ages. The formulation of its intellectual content in the metaphysical terms of Plato and Aristotle occupied the great minds of the philosophers and theologians of the historic Church. Implicit in its teachings are the ethical and social ideals of the dignity and worth of the individual, of human freedom, equality and brotherhood that are the spiritual foundations of a democratic society, and the only possible basis for a world order of peace and good will.

Today this ancient religious heritage of the Western World, together with those ethical and spiritual values which it has created and fostered, faces the greatest challenge in its whole history. It is the challenge of a materialistic, atheistic philosophy that for its adherents has all the emotional drive of a fanatically religious faith. Marxian materialism is far more than an economic system. It is a religion whose fundamental tenets are diametrically opposed to those ideals of Christian faith that are the spiritual foundation of a truly democratic society. In the words of Professor Toynbee, "Communism has been metamorphosed into an emotional and intellectual substitute for orthodox Christianity, with Marx for its Moses, Lenin for its Messiah and their collected works for the Scripture of the new atheistic church."[6] Beneath the surface of the "cold war" between Soviet Russia and the democracies of the West is the profound spiritual issue as to whether the future evolution of human society is to be guided by the atheistic materialism of Karl Marx, or by the

[6] Arnold Toynbee, *A Study of History*, Oxford University Press, New York and London, 1947.

ethical and social ideals implicit in the Idea of God in Man, as revealed in Jesus of Nazareth.

The fiery zeal of the disciples of Marxian materialism is inspired by the profound conviction that their philosophy rests upon an unshakable foundation of truth regarding the nature of human society. The Marxist sees the course of history as bound to follow inevitably the program laid down by Marx and Lenin. For the Communist, it is not a hypothetical God that is on his side. For him the triumph of Communism is assured by the operation of the inexorable economic laws that, according to his philosophy, control the evolution of human society.

In contrast to the dynamic drive of this godless but fanatically religious faith is the uncertainty and doubt in the minds of nominal Christians regarding their own religious beliefs. God is on our side, but we are far from certain that God has much to do with the tide of events in our chaotic world. Our trust is placed rather in the vast material and military resources that we can bring into the gigantic struggle for world supremacy. We maintain a weak and wavering belief in God, but we place our trust in B-36 bombers and an ample stockpile of atomic bombs.

President Conant of Harvard is quoted as saying: "Our fitness to survive as a nation depends upon our making our form of democracy work." It would seem that our almost hysterical fear of Communism within our own borders springs from a haunting anxiety that our form of democracy is not working. Racial discrimination, endless strife between labor and management, the struggle between economic groups over the distribution of material wealth, the presence of dire poverty in the midst of plenty, all conspire to create the uneasy feeling that somehow democracy has got off the track and is bumping along on the ties—that our spiritual strength falls far short of our material greatness.

May it not be that this lack is our inability to bring into practical expression in the conduct of our individual lives and our mechanized society those ideals of human brotherhood, that sense of love and concern for our fellows which are the center and core of the religion we profess, and the only basis for a truly democratic way of life? And may not this failure arise from the fact that we have come to regard these ideals as the pious teachings of an outworn tradition, rather than the expression of truths as deeply rooted in reality as are the truths of material science?

In the foregoing pages we have tried to present a stereoscopic view of what scientifically we know and what as Christians we believe. For the writer such a view validates a belief in a God of love, a personification, if you like, of that mysterious Power that "guides the stars in their courses," and which found expression in finite human terms in the life and death of the Man of Galilee. That belief is not a leap of blind, irrational credulity, but rather a rational faith that gives to both the scientific and the religious quests a spiritual meaning as two approaches to the same goal. Both represent the striving of the spirit of man to transcend the limitations of a purely material, temporal existence—the one to attain a complete understanding of man's physical environment, the other to reach a full recognition of the inner meaning of the conscious creative self.

The questioning scientific mind discovers the Mind of God in the mathematical order that prevails throughout the universe of atoms and stars. The humble trusting heart knows God in the love that lives and grows within itself. The full realization of the free, conscious Self, the *I* that governs and controls under natural laws the atoms of a physical body—that realization comes only with the mystical yet wholly rational experience that God and the atoms and the human soul are *one* in essence, a spiritual trinity, three expressions of the unity of the living Soul of a living universe.

INDEX

INDEX

INDEX